AF807776

Essex Public Library
117 N. Church Ln.
Tappahannock, VA 22560

All About Anime and Manga

The History of Anime and Manga

Andrea C. Nakaya

ReferencePoint Press®

San Diego, CA

ReferencePoint Press®

About the Author

Andrea C. Nakaya, a native of New Zealand, holds a BA in English and an MA in communications from San Diego State University. She has written and edited numerous articles and more than fifty books on current issues. She currently lives in Eagle, Idaho, with her husband and their two children, Natalie and Shane.

© 2022 ReferencePoint Press, Inc.
Printed in the United States

For more information, contact:
ReferencePoint Press, Inc.
PO Box 27779
San Diego, CA 92198
www.ReferencePointPress.com

ALL RIGHTS RESERVED.
No part of this work covered by the copyright hereon may be reproduced or used in any form or by any means—graphic, electronic, or mechanical, including photocopying, recording, taping, web distribution, or information storage retrieval systems—without the written permission of the publisher.

Picture Credits:
Cover: Usa-Pyon/Shutterstock
6: Kyodo/Newscom
9: Kyodo/Newscom
11: Pictures From History/Bridgeman Images
16: Everett Collection/Shutterstock.com
19: Everett Collection/Shutterstock.com
23: Piero Oliosi/Polaris/Newscom
26: United Archives/IFTN/Newscom
29: NBC/Photofest
31: On the road again/Shutterstock
34: Nyuuness/Shutterstock
39: Krikkiat/Shutterstock
41: Photofest
45: Photofest
49: Awana JF/Shutterstock
54: ADD1904/Shutterstock

LIBRARY OF CONGRESS CATALOGING-IN-PUBLICATION DATA

Names: Nakaya, Andrea C., 1976- author.
Title: The history of anime and manga / Andrea C. Nakaya.
Description: San Diego, CA : ReferencePoint Press, 2022. | Series: All about anime and manga | Includes bibliographical references and index.
Identifiers: LCCN 2021030388 (print) | LCCN 2021030389 (ebook) | ISBN 9781678202224 (library binding) | ISBN 9781678202231 (ebook)
Subjects: LCSH: Comic books, strips, etc.--Japan--Juvenile literature. | Animated films--Japan--Juvenile literature. | Animated television programs--Japan--Juvenile literature.
Classification: LCC PN6790.J3 N36 2022 (print) | LCC PN6790.J3 (ebook) | DDC 741.5/952--dc23
LC record available at https://lccn.loc.gov/2021030388
LC ebook record available at https://lccn.loc.gov/2021030389

Contents

Unlike Anything Else

Japan's highest-grossing movie of all time is an anime movie. Released in 2020, *Demon Slayer: Kimetsu no Yaiba the Movie: Mugen Train* is based on a manga series about a boy named Tanjiro, whose family was slaughtered by demons. Tanjiro is on a quest to avenge his family and find a cure for his sister, who was turned into a demon. Not only did *Demon Slayer* become Japan's highest-grossing movie, it was the fourth-highest-grossing movie worldwide for 2020.

Both anime and manga have been popular in Japan for more than one hundred years. More recently, they have also attracted a large number of fans around the world. Manga are comic books and graphic novels that are created in Japan. Unlike most English-language books, they are traditionally read from right to left. Manga series are usually published weekly or monthly in manga magazines. Popular manga are also collected into books. Anime is Japanese animation, and includes television shows and movies. It is often based on existing manga series, as the *Demon Slayer* movie is.

Something for Everyone

Anime and manga are very different from other types of comics and animation. One thing that makes them unique is that they are not just for kids. While many comic books and animated shows developed outside of Japan are aimed mainly at young people, anime and manga are created for all different age groups, from toddlers to adults. In Japan it is common to see kids watching anime shows after school; however, it is also common to see businesspeople on their way to work reading manga comics.

One reason that anime and manga are enjoyed by so many different age groups is that they are very diverse, with stories on a huge variety of topics and levels of maturity. Susan J. Napier teaches Japanese literature and culture at the University of Texas at Austin. She discusses the wide variety of manga, explaining, "Manga cover a dazzling array of topics. These can include child-oriented fare, such as the sports club stories aimed at boys or the highly inventive, beautifully drawn *shōjo* manga produced for young girls, as well as a vast variety of manga for adults ranging from etiquette journals to the so-called Ladies Comic . . . which are actually explicitly erotic comics targeted at women."[1] According to Napier, because there is something to interest everyone, almost everyone in Japan reads manga. Likewise, Napier explains that anime covers a similarly large range of topics and age groups. She says, "Essentially, anime works include everything that Western audiences are accustomed to seeing in live-action films—romance, comedy, tragedy, adventure, even psychological probing of a kind seldom attempted in recent mass-culture Western film or television."[2]

"Manga cover a dazzling array of topics."[1]

—Susan J. Napier, professor of Japanese literature and culture at the University of Texas, Austin

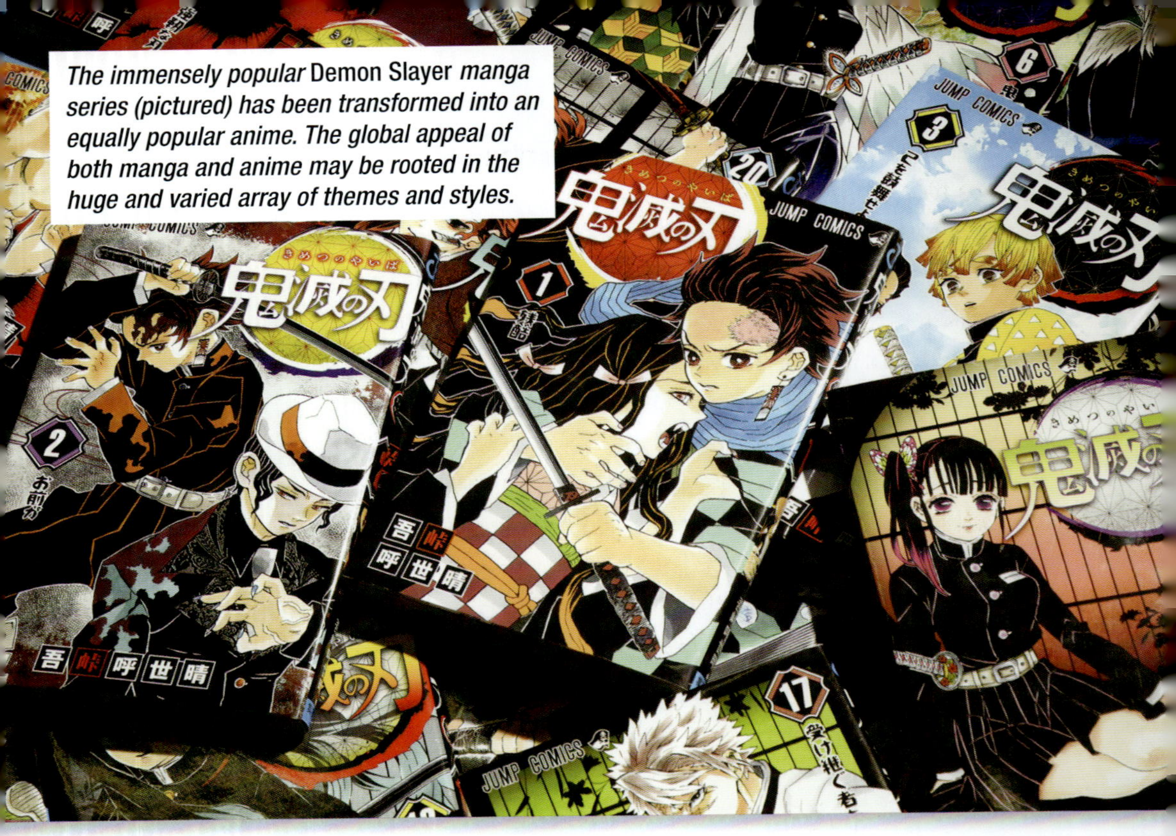

The immensely popular Demon Slayer *manga series (pictured) has been transformed into an equally popular anime. The global appeal of both manga and anime may be rooted in the huge and varied array of themes and styles.*

A Unique Style

Not only are anime and manga extremely diverse, they also have a unique style. One thing that fans quickly notice is that anime and manga characters are often drawn with exaggerated or fantastic physical features or expressions. This can be one way for the artist to show personality or convey what a character is thinking. For instance, huge eyes are very common and make it easier to show emotions. Exaggerated facial expressions are another way to show what characters are thinking. For example, a person who is embarrassed or angry might have a completely red face. Many anime and manga characters also have crazy, unnaturally colored hair. An example of this is Yugi, from *Yu-Gi-Oh!*, who stands out with spiky, blond bangs that look like lightning bolts and has larger black and purple spikes at the back of his head. Akari, a character from *Yuri Yuri*, has hair that helps protect her; two small hair buns on the sides of her head can detach and fire at an enemy in an attack called Bun Bazooka.

Manga and anime also use a number of unique visual techniques to convey messages about what is happening in the story. Japanese popular culture expert Patrick Drazen explains a common one, saying, "Perhaps the most distinctive convention is the tendency, in moments of action or high emotion, for the background to vanish entirely. Instead, we see broad sweeping lines suggesting speed or power." Drazen explains that this technique is used to tell the reader or viewer something important about a character. "This device focuses our attention on the character, but also cues us that the character is engaged in a major struggle or effort,"[3] he says. While those new to manga and anime might not understand the significance of visual cues such as this, for those who do understand them, these cues add a deeper layer of meaning to the story.

> **"Characters like Astro Boy, Speed Racer, and Sailor Moon have become as ubiquitous as Mickey Mouse."[4]**
>
> —Japan House, which promotes Japanese art, technology, and innovation

An Important Cultural Export

Anime and manga have been a staple form of entertainment in Japan for many years, and while they took a while to catch on outside of Japan, they have ultimately become one of the country's most popular exports. Japan House, a project that works to further awareness and appreciation of a number of different forms of Japanese art, technology, and innovation, says that manga and anime have become an important cultural influence around the globe. It explains, "[Anime and manga] characters like Astro Boy, Speed Racer, and Sailor Moon have become as ubiquitous as Mickey Mouse, adorning backpacks, toys, and lunchboxes worldwide."[4] Every year, these and many more characters attract hundreds of thousands of passionate fans all over the world.

Chapter One

Early Anime and Manga

Long before Japanese artists were drawing manga and anime characters, the Japanese people were using pictures as a way to express ideas. For example, kanji was the first Japanese writing system to be developed, and it is based on pictures. Each kanji character—or ideogram—is like a simple picture that represents a particular word. The pictogram for *mountain* looks like the three peaks of a mountain range, and the one for *tree* looks like the trunk of a tree. Susan J. Napier explains that visual imagery is very important in Japanese culture, a culture she describes as "pictocentric." She says, "Japan is a country that is traditionally more pictocentric than the cultures of the West." This focus on the visual is one reason that anime and manga are so popular there. She says, "Anime and manga fit easily into a contemporary culture of the visual."[5] As illustrated by kanji, that culture of the visual has long been a part of Japan. It has influenced the birth and development of both manga and anime and is one of the reasons that these art forms remain so popular there today.

The Origins of Manga

Manga—and all comics—are created using a process called sequential art, in which drawings and sometimes words are shown in sequence across a page in order to tell a story. Many people believe that the first example of sequential art in Japan was in the twelfth century, when Buddhist monks created sequential illustrations on scrolls. Many different scrolls were created by the monks, but the most famous are the *Chōju Giga*, also called "animal scrolls," which contain pictures of animals acting like humans. Robin E. Brenner is a librarian and an expert on anime and manga. She describes these scrolls, saying, "The *Chōju Giga* feature a lengthy sequence of expressive and humorous scenes of animals, including monkeys, foxes, rabbits, and toads, acting out the activities and pastimes of members of the clergy and the nobility." The scrolls were viewed from right to left, and according to Brenner, they stretched as far

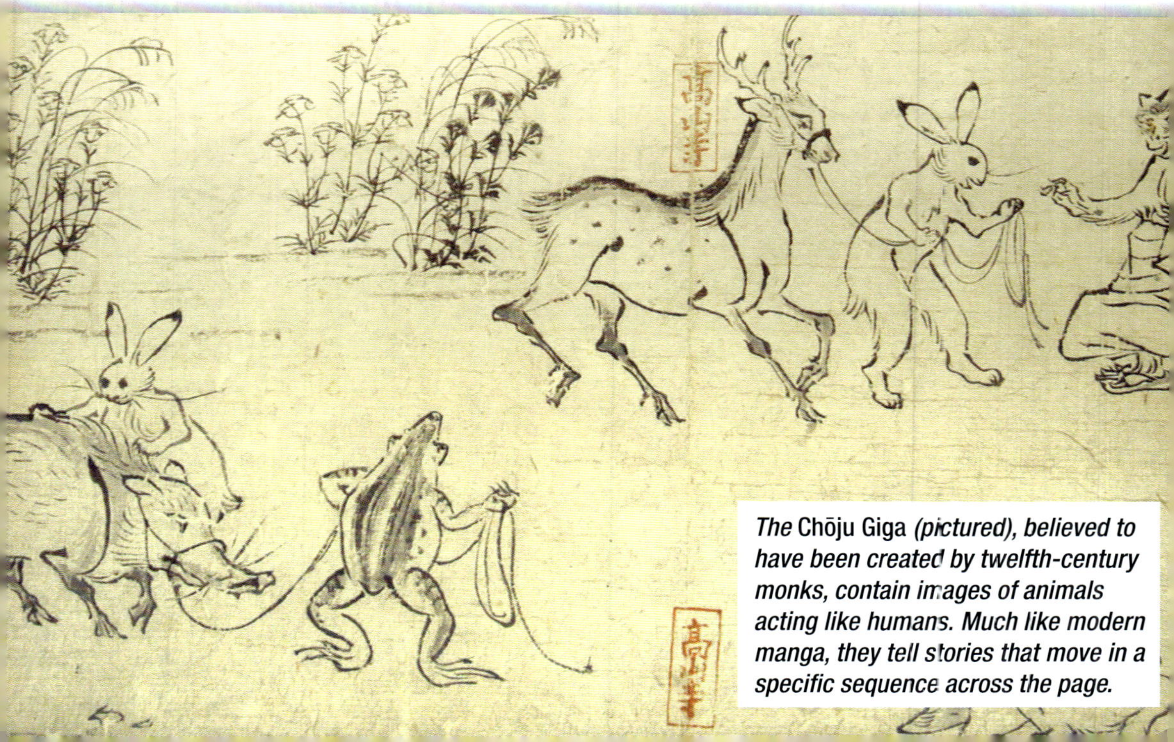

The Chōju Giga *(pictured), believed to have been created by twelfth-century monks, contain images of animals acting like humans. Much like modern manga, they tell stories that move in a specific sequence across the page.*

"The *Chōju Giga* feature a lengthy sequence of expressive and humorous scenes of animals, including monkeys, foxes, rabbits, and toads, acting out the activities and pastimes of members of the clergy and the nobility."[6]

—Robin E. Brenner, a librarian and an expert on anime and manga

as 80 feet (24.4 m). "Most important to the history of manga," she adds, "they follow a definite sequence across the page to tell their story and thus lay the pattern for sequential storytelling to come."[6] She says that the monks continued to make scrolls for hundreds of years on religious topics, as well as on other themes such as ghosts or even more crude subject matter such as men having farting contests.

Woodblock printing was another early precursor to manga. This type of art involves carving an image into a piece of wood, then using ink to reproduce it on a piece of paper. During the early 1600s to the late 1800s—a period of time referred to as the Tokugawa, or Edo period—a style of woodblock printing called *ukiyo-e*, or "pictures of the floating world," became popular. Ukiyo-e prints originally showed the various different entertainments enjoyed by the wealthy, such as brothels, theaters, and teahouses. However, later they also contained pictures of everyday life. Because a woodblock print could be reproduced many times, the prints became a cheap and popular form of mass entertainment, just as manga later would. In an online article about ukiyo-e art, one author talks about the many similarities between ukiyo-e and manga, stating:

> The woodblock prints at the time of their creation were affordable, targeted at a mass audience and served the popular taste of the day, much like today's manga volumes and magazines. Moreover, there is a thematic similarity in that both genres explore themes of sex, violence, the op-

position between rich/powerful, and poor/powerless, heroes vs. villains, supernatural phenomena and Japanese folklore legends.[7]

Early Manga

There is disagreement about when the word *manga* was first used to describe collections of images. Some people believe it was first used in 1798 to describe a book of pictures called *Four Seasons* by artist Santō Kyōden. His pictures included creatures from Japanese legends. Others maintain that the artist Katsushika Hokusai was the first to use the word *manga* for images. In 1814 he published a book of drawings that he called *Hokusai Manga*. Unlike the manga that would come later, Kyōden's and Hokusai's books did not tell a story. Instead, they were simply collections of sketches.

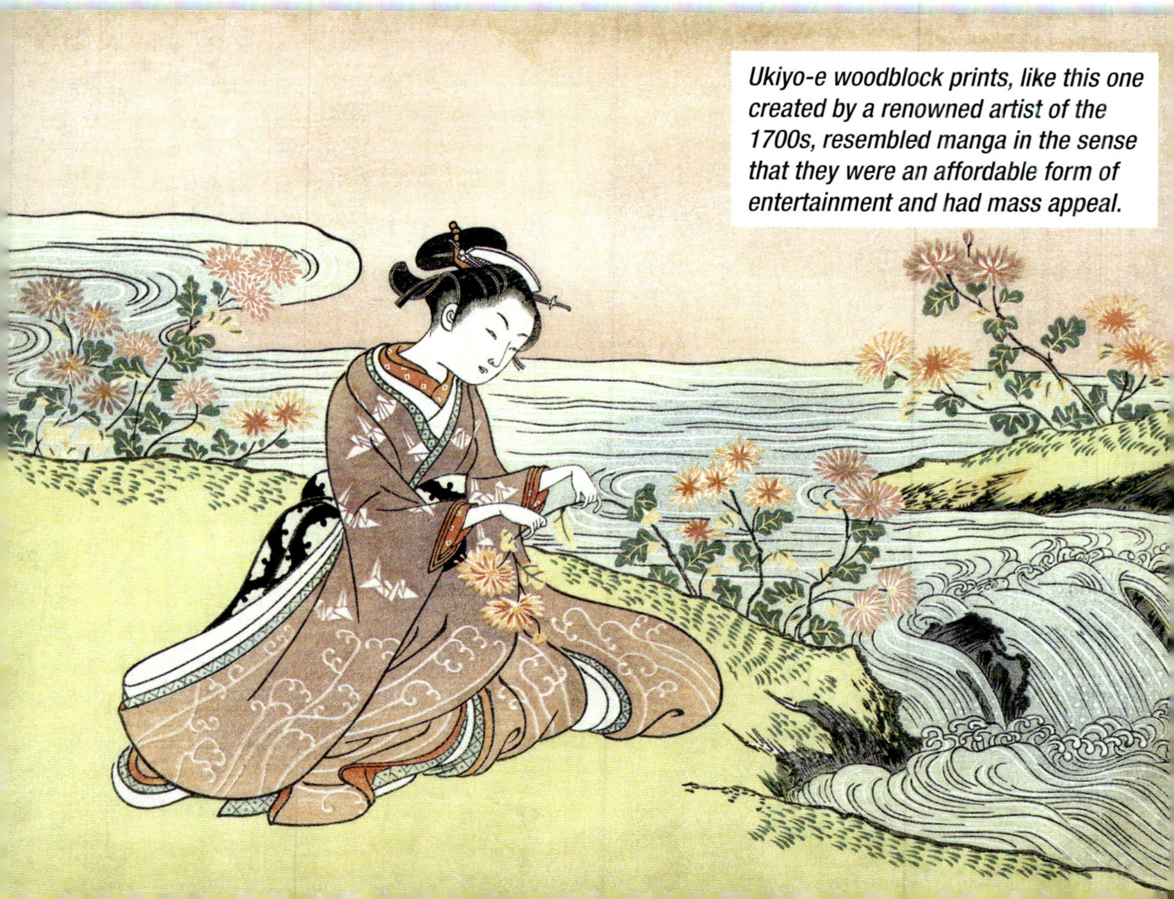

Ukiyo-e woodblock prints, like this one created by a renowned artist of the 1700s, resembled manga in the sense that they were an affordable form of entertainment and had mass appeal.

Soon artists began to put images together into actual stories that were more like the manga that exist today. By the late eighteenth century, bound books of cartoons were being created in Japan. Some of these early books were called *kibyōshi*, or "yellow books." Manga expert Christy C. says, "Kibyōshi were possibly the first recognizable ancestor of modern Japanese comic book because of their small book form and their release as serials (often with two or three volumes per series). They consisted of images throughout the pages with writing occupying much of the empty space."[8] She notes that kibyōshi were written for adults, and the images, topics, and plots in them were often mature in nature.

Japanese art and artists experienced influences from abroad beginning in the 1850s. After more than two hundred years of isolation, this is when Japan finally gave in to pressure from the United States and other countries to open up to contact and trade with the Western world. These influences had an impact on manga. Japanese artists were exposed to art from other countries, including comic strips and political cartoons, and this gave them new ideas and techniques that they incorporated into their own work. For example, many artists began to include shading, perspective, and speech bubbles. Serial comics and comics that satirized culture and politics also became popular. A well-known comic magazine was *Japan Punch*, published from 1862 to 1887. This magazine had cartoons that satirized Westerners in Japan.

"Kibyōshi were possibly the first recognizable ancestor of modern Japanese comic book because of their small book form and their release as serials."[8]

—Christy C., an expert on manga

The first magazines dedicated exclusively to manga were released in the late 1800s. *Eshinbun Nipponshi* was first; it was released in 1874, but only three issues were ever published. Other magazines followed. In 1895 the first *shonen* magazine, *Syōnen*

Narrators of Early Anime

Early anime films were silent, since when anime was first made, filmmakers did not yet know how to put sound in a film. To make up for the lack of sound, most films had a narrator, or *benshi*, standing by the screen to narrate. Writer Michael Richey explains the purpose and the importance of the narrator:

> When film began to spread throughout Japan, rather than accepting it as an evolution of photography as the west did, it was viewed as an extension of theater. Since kabuki, noh, and bunraku theater traditions all had narrators, naturally film needed one as well. Enter the benshi, a narrator who not only read aloud the onscreen intertitles, but also described the film's events in real time and gave voice to each and every character.

This means that the early silent anime that still exist are incomplete because, as Richey notes, they do not have the benshi narration that was such an important part of the film.

Michael Richey, "Anime Before It Was 'Anime,'" *Tofugu* (blog), April 9, 2014. www.tofugu.com.

Sekai, was published. Syōnen is a type of manga that is aimed at teenage boys. At this time, Japan was at war with China, and the new magazine had stories about bravery during times of war. Despite the publication of early magazines such as these, it was not until World War II ended in 1945 that manga magazines really started to become popular in Japan.

The First Anime

Japan's first anime was made in the early 1900s. Unfortunately, most of it no longer exists. This is because the material that early films were made on was not long lasting, and many early films deteriorated quickly. In addition, films were often intentionally taken apart after they were shown. Finally, many early films were destroyed in a

1923 earthquake and in the bombing that happened during World War II. Since most early anime was destroyed, historians are unsure about exactly what came first. Some people believe that the very first anime was a filmstrip that was discovered in 2005 and is believed to have been created in 1907. It shows a boy in a sailor uniform drawing the characters for *moving picture* on a blackboard. The fragment is named *Katsudō Shashin*, which means "moving picture." Other people believe that the first anime film was actually created in 1917. However, there is disagreement over exactly which film that was, because more than one was made that year. Two possibilities include a film called *Bumpy New Picture Book—Failure of a Great Plan* and another with the title *The Story of the Concierge Mukuzo Imokawa*.

"While the films looked different, the content would be familiar to anyone who watches anime today. They told funny stories about samurai, brought Japanese folk tales to life, and promoted the Japanese mail system."[9]

—Right Stuf Inc., a video publisher and distributor

All of the early anime films were very short—most likely less than five minutes—and were silent, although when they were screened they were probably accompanied by live music and a narrator. They were created by drawing a picture with chalk, filming it, then erasing the picture and drawing a new one for the next shot. With this technique, it took a long time to create even a short film. Yet while the early anime techniques were different from today, as video publisher and distributor Right Stuf Inc. points out, that anime actually resembled present-day anime in many ways. The company says, "While the films looked different, the content would be familiar to anyone who watches anime today. They told funny stories about samurai, brought Japanese folk tales to life, and promoted the Japanese mail system. It's a line-up you could find in just about any year of the last decade."[9]

Images Matter

Kitazawa Rakuten was a Japanese artist who played an important role in the early development of manga. Kitazawa was born in 1876. He is known for creating humorous comic strips that criticized the government and society, and in 1905 he founded the satirical magazine *Tokyo Puck*. According to a column posted on the Comics Forum website, Kitazawa believed that the images were the most important part of manga. The author explains, "Kitazawa . . . asserts that manga should ideally have a minimal amount of words, and cartoonists 'should endeavor to make the pictures speak.' For him this applied equally to single-panel cartoons and multi-panel comic strips: he opined that comic strips that make the reader 'perceive the story without explanation are best.'" In addition to the manga he created, Kitazawa is also known for being the first person to start a school in Japan that specialized in comics and caricature. He taught at the school from 1934, when it first opened, until 1948, when he retired. In 1955 he passed away at age seventy-nine.

Ronald Stewart, "Manga Studies #2: Manga History: Shimizu Isao and Miyamoto Hirohito on Japan's First Modern 'Manga' Artist Kitazawa Rakuten," Comics Forum, June 14, 2014. https://comicsforum.org.

Three of the early pioneering anime filmmakers were Ōten Shimokawa, Jun'ichi Kōuchi, and Seitarō Kitayama. Before he made anime, Kitayama was a painter, and the other two began as manga artists. These three men produced a large number of anime in the early years of the medium, and for that reason, some people call them the "fathers" of anime. One of the oldest of their films that survived is called *The Dull Sword*, a two-minute film by Kōuchi about a samurai who buys a dull sword and is then defeated because the sword is useless.

As technology developed, there were a lot of firsts in the early years of anime. For example, artists learned how to create films with sound. The first anime film with prerecorded, synced voices was the 1933 *Within the World of Power and Women*, about a man who gets tired of his overbearing wife and has an affair with his secretary. In the early years of anime, there was also a major change in the way that it was drawn. Filmmakers switched to cel technology—*cel* is short for "celluloid." With cel technology, artists no longer had to draw and redraw chalk images. Instead, they painted on transparent sheets of celluloid, which could then be layered on top of one another. This new technique was more expensive but also quicker and easier to use. *The Dance of Chagamas*, a 1953 film about a group of tanukis (Japanese raccoon dogs) causing mischief, is believed to be the first anime created completely with cels. It is six minutes long.

Early anime films were made for existing Japanese film companies, but that changed in 1921 with another industry first. That year, Kitayama created the first anime film studio. He named it Kitayama Eiga Seisakujo. This new studio did not survive very long; much of it was destroyed by the 1923 earthquake, which at the time was considered the worst natural disaster in Japanese history. However, while the studio lasted only two years, many of its animators continued to create anime. Also, the idea of a studio that exclusively made anime was there to stay, and there would be many more in the future.

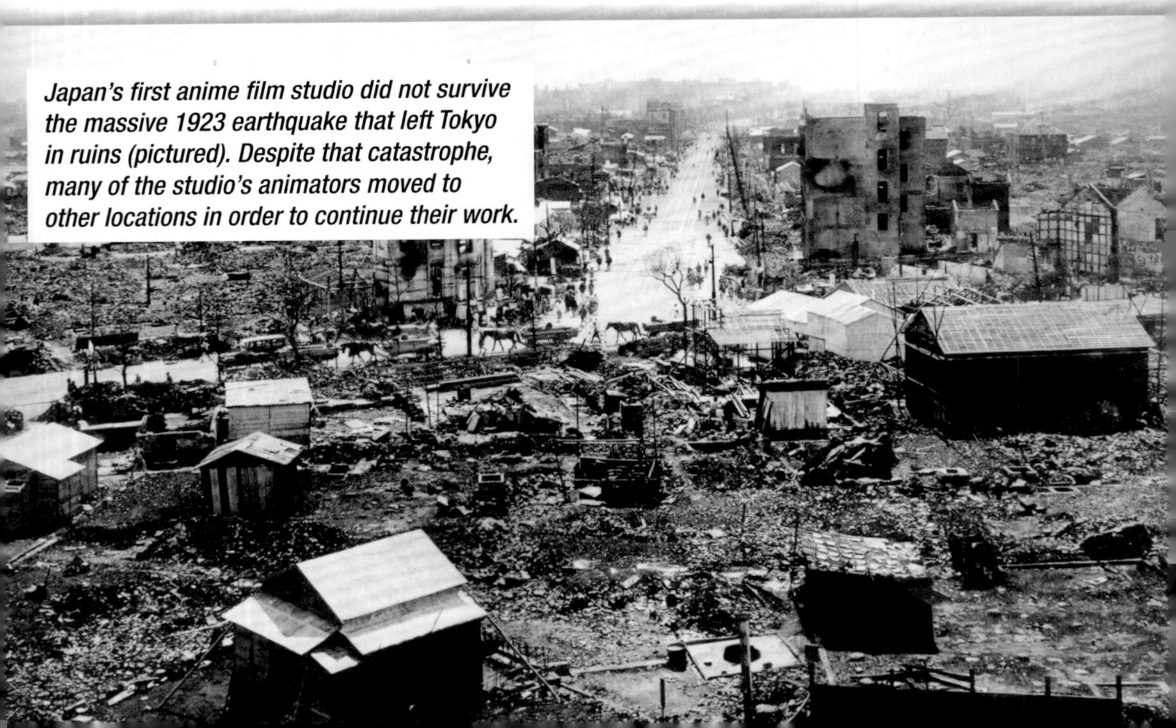

Japan's first anime film studio did not survive the massive 1923 earthquake that left Tokyo in ruins (pictured). Despite that catastrophe, many of the studio's animators moved to other locations in order to continue their work.

World War II and Censorship

In 1939 manga and anime artists suddenly faced some drastic changes. That was the year that World War II began, with Japan entering the conflict the next year. World War II had a significant impact on the development of both manga and anime, because it stifled much of the creative development that had been happening up until that time. Suddenly, artists were no longer free to create whatever they wanted. Their work was often censored by the government. Some were even arrested for producing work that the government did not like. Liana Sharer, author on the website That Anime Project, explains that as a result of this censorship, artists changed what they did. For instance, she says, "Many magazines either closed or started censoring themselves harshly; magazines who did neither frequently had their editors arrested. These types of arrests happened so often that magazines would sometimes pick an employee to be a 'jail editor' who would have the honor of taking the punishment and saving his company."[10] In the face of restriction and intimidation, many artists stopped creating manga and anime altogether during the war.

Others chose to put their talents toward making propaganda for the government. The creation of propaganda was not unique to Japan; many nations produced propaganda to encourage public support for their war effort. The first feature-length anime film created in Japan was a propaganda film. Titled *Momotaro: Sacred Sailors*, it was commissioned by Japan's navy and released in 1945. The film is seventy-four minutes long and portrays the sailors as brave monkeys, rabbits, bears, and other animals. Just as the United States used racist stereotypes in its own propaganda, *Momotaro* contains racist depictions of Caucasians, showing them in human form but with big, floppy bodies and huge noses.

While this film was a milestone in the history of anime, overall, World War II was not a time of significant growth for the anime or manga industries. However, this stagnation was only a temporary pause until the war ended.

Chapter Two

Development After World War II

Space Battleship Yamato is an anime series that premiered in Japan in 1974. It is set in the year 2199, after an alien race has destroyed the surface of the earth with radioactive bombs. People on earth create a spaceship from the ruins of a Japanese battleship called *Yamato* and travel into space on a mission to find the device that can reverse the radiation. While it was created years after World War II ended, *Space Battleship Yamato* takes its name from something that happened during the war. *Yamato* was a Japanese Navy battleship that was sunk in the East China Sea in 1945. The series is just one example of how the events of World War II had a significant impact on the people of Japan, including the artists of manga and anime. Many artists were deeply influenced by the violence, loss of life, and suppression of freedoms that came with the war. However, when the war ended, these artists were also greatly affected by the sudden freedom they were given when many restrictions were lifted and there was suddenly tremendous opportunity for growth and creativity. Overall, the end of the war was a turning point in the development of both manga and anime.

How the End of the War Influenced Manga and Anime

The violence and death that Japan experienced as a result of World War II have had a lasting impact on the manga and anime that have been created since then. Japan fought in the war for five years, during which time millions of Japanese died. The country surrendered in 1945, after the United States dropped atomic bombs on the cities of Hiroshima and Nagasaki. This was the first and only time that an atomic bomb has been used in warfare, and

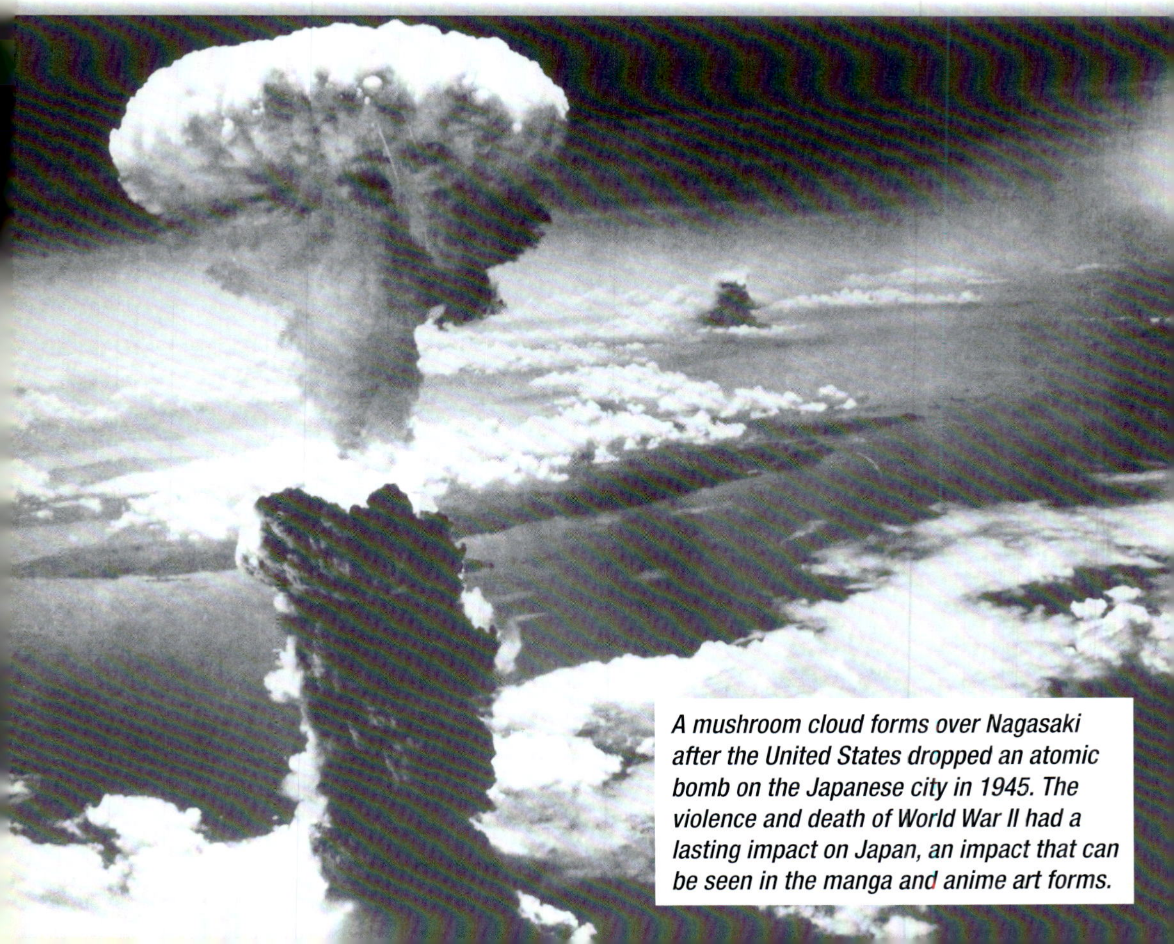

A mushroom cloud forms over Nagasaki after the United States dropped an atomic bomb on the Japanese city in 1945. The violence and death of World War II had a lasting impact on Japan, an impact that can be seen in the manga and anime art forms.

the destruction and loss of life was horrific. The two cities were largely destroyed, tens of thousands of people were killed instantly, and tens of thousands more suffered from burns and radiation poisoning. The bombing was so traumatizing to the people of Japan that it has had a lasting effect on their culture, and this includes manga and anime. Librarian and manga expert Robin E. Brenner explains, "Many of the most common themes in manga and anime today can be traced to the war and the bombs, from the examination of the conflict between man and technology to the threat of apocalypse in the stories. Most notably, of course, are the strong antiwar messages often found in postwar anime and manga."[11] These antiwar messages and fears of an apocalypse are a result of all the ways that Japan suffered in the war.

"Many of the most common themes in manga and anime today can be traced to the war and the bombs."[11]

—Robin E. Brenner, a librarian and manga expert

While the war ended with these horrific bombings, the end of the war did eventually bring many new freedoms to the people of Japan. With the war over, the previous restrictions on anime and manga were lifted, and artists were again free to create without fear of censorship or intimidation. In addition, because so many artists had been afraid to work during the war, after the war there was more opportunity than ever before for people to create manga and anime. As a result, the end of the war was a time of growth for both anime and manga. Existing artists created again, new artists emerged, and there were new series, new ideas, and new manga publishers and anime studios.

Foreign Influence

The end of the war also led to another period of foreign influence on Japanese culture, and that too affected the development of manga and anime. After its defeat in the war, Japan was occupied by the United States from 1945 to 1952. During that occu-

Why Manga Is Black and White

Early on, both anime and manga were only created in black and white. Over time, technology changed, and most anime is now produced in color; however, most manga are still printed in black and white. Cost is one reason; black-and-white manga are cheaper to produce than color. Time is another reason. Manga creation is time consuming. Most manga artists already work long hours to meet their deadlines. Adding color would slow that process.

Artist David Fox sees another reason for keeping manga black and white. In his view it is artistically superior to color manga. He explains, "Reading through a black and white manga is just [like] watching a really well done black and white movie. It conveys a certain mood, especially in the use of shadows, much better than color could." Further, he says, the use of only black and white pushes artists to develop better artistic techniques in order to convey their desired message. He says, "Over the last few decades manga artists have developed plenty of excellent techniques of using black-and-white art to make their manga unique pieces of art."

David Fox, "The Cultural Significance of Manga and Anime," *David Charles Fox* (blog), December 27, 2018. https://davidcharlesfox.com.

pation Japanese artists were exposed to American comics and cartoons. They discovered new styles and ideas and incorporated some of these into their own art. Disney, in particular, made a big impression, and many Japanese artists started to try some of the same techniques that they saw in Disney movies, such as characters with big eyes and exaggerated expressions. Combining foreign influences such as Disney with their own artistic techniques, Japanese artists began to create styles that were new.

One of the first people to do this was a man named Osamu Tezuka. Tezuka was born in Osaka, Japan, in 1928, and started drawing as a child. After the war, he quickly became a prolific and famous creator of manga and then anime. Blogger Tabatha Butler explains how Tezuka combined ideas from Disney with his own style to create something completely new. She says, "Of course, Tezuka created all of his own characters and story lines, but he borrowed the bold lines, round heads and large, expressive eyes of Disney characters, making his own characters at once impossibly cute and extremely expressive."[12] Akihiro Kanayama, who worked as an animator with Tezuka, says that Tezuka took ideas from many different places. He explains, "Tezuka was filled with curiosity. He'd look at comic media from all over the world. Of course he loved Disney, but he found things from France, from Italy . . . all these places, and he'd find elements he liked and make use of them."[13]

The God of Manga

Tezuka's new style revolutionized both manga and anime. One unique element that he introduced into manga was the use of cinematic techniques like panning and zooming, which helped create the feeling of movement. One expert explains, "His cinematic style and frame-by-frame action created a sense of drama not present in earlier 4 panel manga. By bringing his readers into the action, Tezuka's work changed the way audiences connected to manga and created a visual story-telling art form the effects of which can still be seen today."[14] Another way Tezuka changed the manga industry was by creating long-running stories that stretched out over many different comic strips, which helped keep the attention of fans. He was a prolific artist and created more than seven hundred manga series over the course of his life. He is even said to have continued to draw manga from his hospital bed, right before his death in 1989. Tezuka also created

"Tezuka was filled with curiosity. He'd look at comic media from all over the world . . . and he'd find elements he liked and make use of them."[13]

—Akihiro Kanayama, an animator who worked with Osamu Tezuka

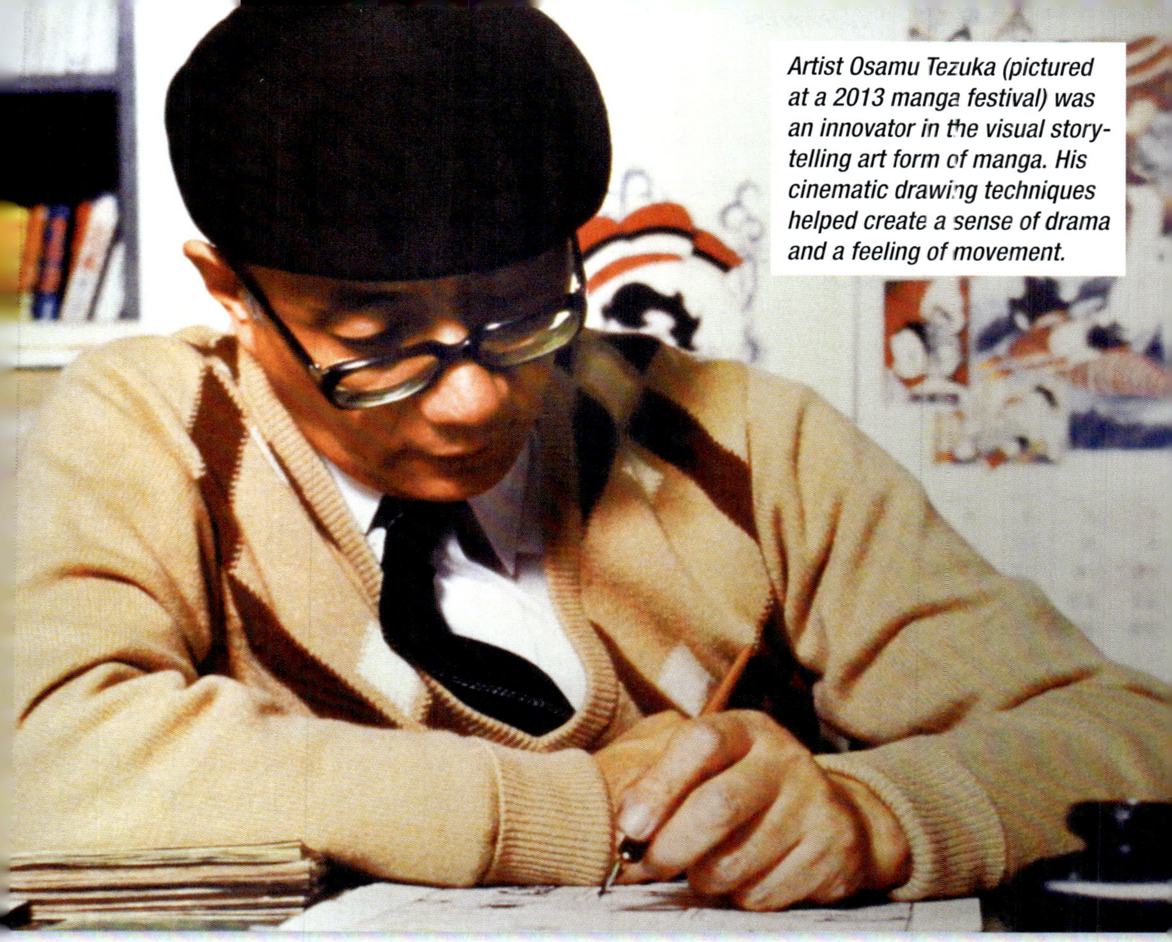

Artist Osamu Tezuka (pictured at a 2013 manga festival) was an innovator in the visual storytelling art form of manga. His cinematic drawing techniques helped create a sense of drama and a feeling of movement.

many anime and was very influential in that field too. In fact, he founded Mushi Production, one of Japan's early animation studios, and many of the films and shows that the studio produced were based on his manga.

Tezuka was so influential that many people call him the "father" or "god" of manga. Without him, manga and anime would be far different than they are today. Frederik L. Schodt is a translator who worked with Tezuka. He says, "I have met many famous and talented people in the course of my career as a professional interpreter, but I have never met anyone quite as unforgettable as Tezuka. He was a man extraordinary for his imagination, intellect, and productivity—a bundle of curiosity, and a cauldron of constantly fermenting ideas."[15] Tezuka has inspired countless other artists and millions of fans all over the world.

Becoming a Mangaka

In Japan, a manga artist is known as a *mangaka*. Spaniard Héctor Garcia has written a number of books about his experiences living and working in Japan. One topic he explores is how an artist becomes a mangaka. He explains there are a number of ways for this to happen. An artist can attend a manga school, where he or she can learn how to create manga. Or, as is common, the aspiring mangaka can work as an assistant to an established artist, or sensei. "In the mangaka's studio, there are usually several assistants to help draw backgrounds and other details. They almost always remain anonymous and very often work as trainees," Garcia explains. This is the preferred route. He continues, "For young artists, this is a good way to enter the profession, since the art of manga has to be learned under the tutelage of a sensei . . . and through constant repetition and ceaseless practice until the students outdo their teachers."

Héctor Garcia, *A Geek in Japan*. Tokyo: Tuttle, 2010, p. 105.

Manga After the War

While Tezuka is one of the most well-known manga artists from this time period, he was not the only one. After World War II many new manga artists emerged. At that time, most people in Japan did not have a lot of money, and manga became popular because it was a cheap form of entertainment that almost everyone could enjoy. Small manga books with red covers, printed on cheap paper and called "red books," became popular. One popular red book was *New Treasure Island*, started in 1947 by Tezuka. It follows a boy named Pete, whose father dies and leaves him a map to a treasure island. For people who wanted to read *New Treasure Island* and other manga but could not afford to actually buy them, there was another option called *kashibonya*. Kashibonya were pay libraries that would lend out manga comics for a small fee.

After World War II, a growing number of weekly manga magazines were also established. For example, *Weekly Shōnen Magazine* started in 1959. It was not the first manga magazine; however, it is important to the history of manga. This magazine established the format that others would follow, inspired similar ventures, and helped grow the popularity of manga among the Japanese public. According to one expert, "1959 is seen as Japan's start to a comic explosion. This is the year when the comic industry was 'jolted' by *Shonen Magazine*, which would eventually grow to 300-page publication."[16] Within a few years of *Weekly Shōnen Magazine*'s debut, seven new weekly comic magazines began publication, five aimed at boys and two targeting girls. *Weekly Shōnen Magazine* is still published and is one of the most popular manga magazines in Japan and around the world. The majority of its readers are males in high school and college.

Anime After the War

Anime took a bit longer than manga to catch on, but catch on it did. In 1956 Hiroshi Ōkawa, the head of the Tōei film company, founded the first modern animation studio, Tōei Dōga (renamed Tōei Animation in 1998). Like Tezuka, Ōkawa is said to have been inspired by Disney—in particular, the company's 1937 animated movie *Snow White*. According to experts, he wanted to make films that rivaled Disney. He even hoped to be seen one day as the Disney of the East. Toward this end, anime industry veteran Yasuo Yamaguchi says, "In 1956, he built a modern studio—a white-walled palace with air conditioning, as people called it—and founded Tōei Dōga." The studio's filmmakers spent a lot of time learning exactly how Disney created its animation. Yamaguchi explains, "Tōei Dōga chose *Hakujaden* (The Legend of the White Snake) as their first film. They sent a research team to the United States and invited several experts to travel to Japan as mentors. As a result, they were able to master the Disney system of 'assembly-line production.'"[17] *The Legend of the White Snake* was Japan's first feature-length color anime film, and it won international film festival awards. Tōei Animation—the company that created it—still exists and has produced many popular anime, including *Sailor Moon* and *Dragon Ball Z*.

Making animated films is a very labor-intensive process. By the early 2000s most anime studios had started using computer programs to speed up the process, but in the early days of anime, there was no such thing, and it took a long time to create every show and movie. An anime blogger who goes by the name Washi describes the process before the use of computers, explaining, "Prior to around 2000 each drawing had to be replicated onto transparent cel sheets, painstaking hand-painted, and then mounted in as a layer in a machine called the animation stand.

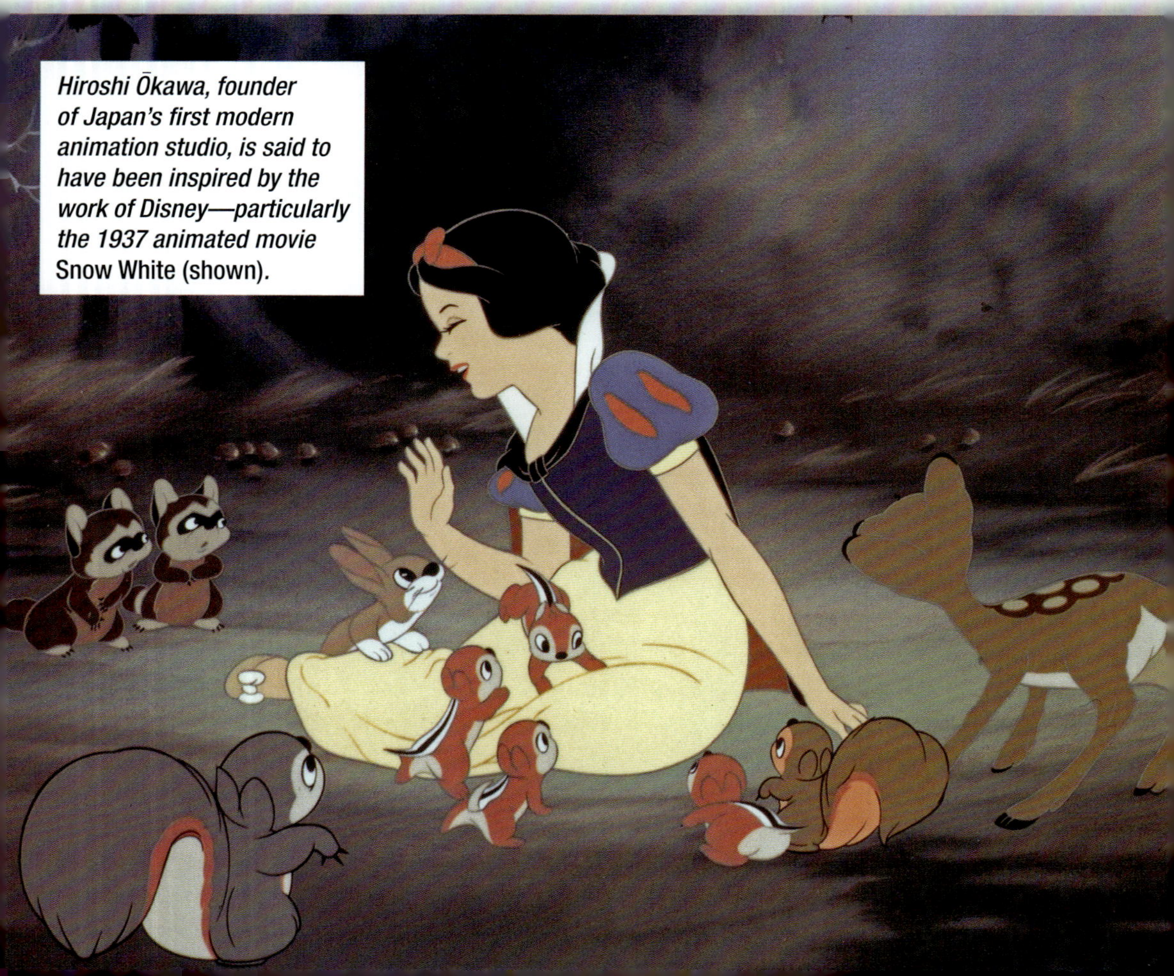

Hiroshi Ōkawa, founder of Japan's first modern animation studio, is said to have been inspired by the work of Disney—particularly the 1937 animated movie **Snow White (shown).**

The stand allowed for the layers to be composited, lit and filmed frame by frame." All of this work required a large staff. Typically, the studio hired men for certain jobs and women for others. For example, Washi states, "while the animation department was almost entirely staffed by males, the tracing/painting department of Toei was largely comprised of women, and lower paid. It was thought that women had a better eye for colour, while men were better inclined to the draftsmanship needed for animation."[18]

"Tōei Dōga chose *Hakujaden* (The Legend of the White Snake) as their first film. They sent a research team to the United States and invited several experts to travel to Japan as mentors."[17]

—Yasuo Yamaguchi, an anime industry veteran

Overall, both manga and anime went through some significant changes after World War II. When the war and its restrictions ended, artists were once again free to innovate, and they did just that, combining foreign influences such as Disney with their own styles. New artists, new series, and new publishers and animation studios all came into being. And the Japanese public was an eager audience for all of these new creations.

Chapter Three

Growth During the 1960s and 1970s

On January 1, 1963, an anime about a robot boy premiered on Japanese TV. The show was called *Tetsuwan Atom*, or *Mighty Atom*—later named *Astro Boy*. It begins with a mad scientist creating a boy robot with human emotions. The robot is intended to replace his own son, who died in a car accident. The scientist soon realizes that the robot, whom he names Astro Boy, will never replace his son, and so he sells him to a circus. Luckily, Astro Boy is rescued by the kind Professor Ochanomizu, who teaches him to respect both people and robots. This is the beginning of many adventures in which Astro Boy uses his super abilities to fight all kinds of threats.

Astro Boy was unlike anything that the Japanese people had ever seen, and they instantly loved it. It marked the beginning of a period of significant growth and development for both anime and manga.

Throughout the 1960s and 1970s, artists created many new series and genres of comic books, television shows, and movies, ranging from science fiction to stories about everyday life.

Astro Boy and Anime on TV

The growing popularity of television was a turning point in the history of anime, because animators started to create new types of content specifically for television. Before 1960 people in Japan watched animation in movie theaters. However, starting in the 1960s televisions began to become popular in Japanese homes, and one of the types of shows that people could watch was anime. At first, television anime shows were similar to what people had already seen in theaters. They were relatively short and were generally not made up of multiple episodes like anime are today. For example, *Mole's Adventure*, released in 1958, was the first anime to be shown on Japanese TV. It is about nine minutes in

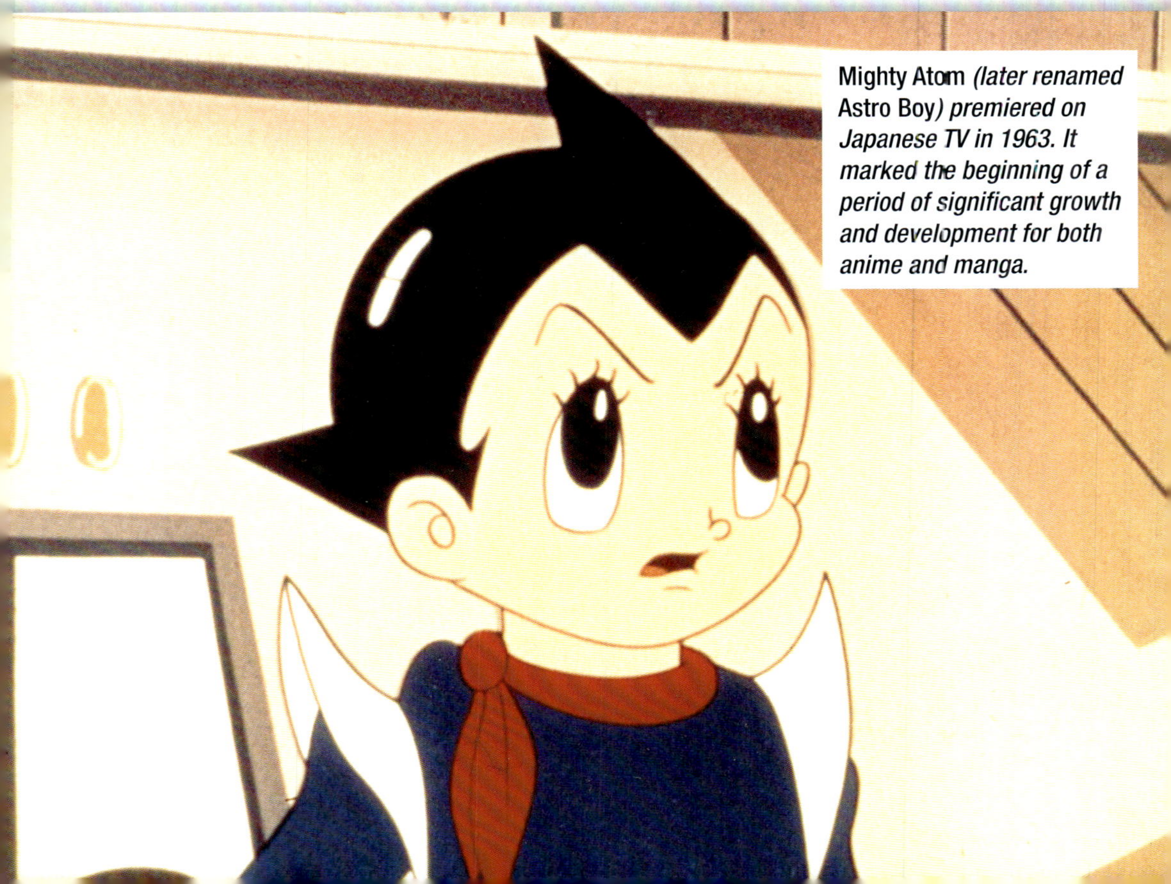

Mighty Atom *(later renamed* Astro Boy*) premiered on Japanese TV in 1963. It marked the beginning of a period of significant growth and development for both anime and manga.*

length and is about a mole who falls asleep and travels through space in his dreams, meeting aliens that live on a strange planet.

In 1963 Osamu Tezuka changed all of that with his new show, *Astro Boy*. Tezuka originally worked for the animation studio Tōei Dōga, but in 1961 he formed his own studio, Mushi Production. Mushi Production's first television series was *Tetsuwan Atom*, and it marked the beginning of a new type of anime. The show was based on a popular manga of the same name created by Tezuka, which was published between 1952 and 1968. What made Tezuka's *Astro Boy* anime different from other anime on television was that it was thirty minutes long. Video publisher and distributor Right Stuf Inc. explains the significance of this, saying, "Anime had never been tried on TV in a half-hour timeslot before due to cost and deadline concerns. How could such a time-intensive process ever be used to profitably air a show a week?"[19] Right Stuf Inc. explains that Tezuka found various different solutions to this problem, including reusing animation cels, having fewer frames per second, and layering cels so that he did not need to redraw everything for each frame.

"Many tropes we think of when we think 'anime' today were codified by *Tetsuwan Atom*, including big eyes, robot battles, and stylized hair impossible to achieve in normal gravity."[20]

—Right Stuf Inc., a video publisher and distributor

His idea was an instant success and set a new standard for anime on television. Not only did *Astro Boy* establish the idea of having anime shows that were thirty minutes long, with recurring episodes, it was also hugely influential in the style of animation that came after it. The Right Stuf Inc. says, "Many tropes we think of when we think 'anime' today were codified by *Tetsuwan Atom*, including big eyes, robot battles, and stylized hair impossible to achieve in normal gravity. It was the coolest thing on TV and everyone loved it!"[20]

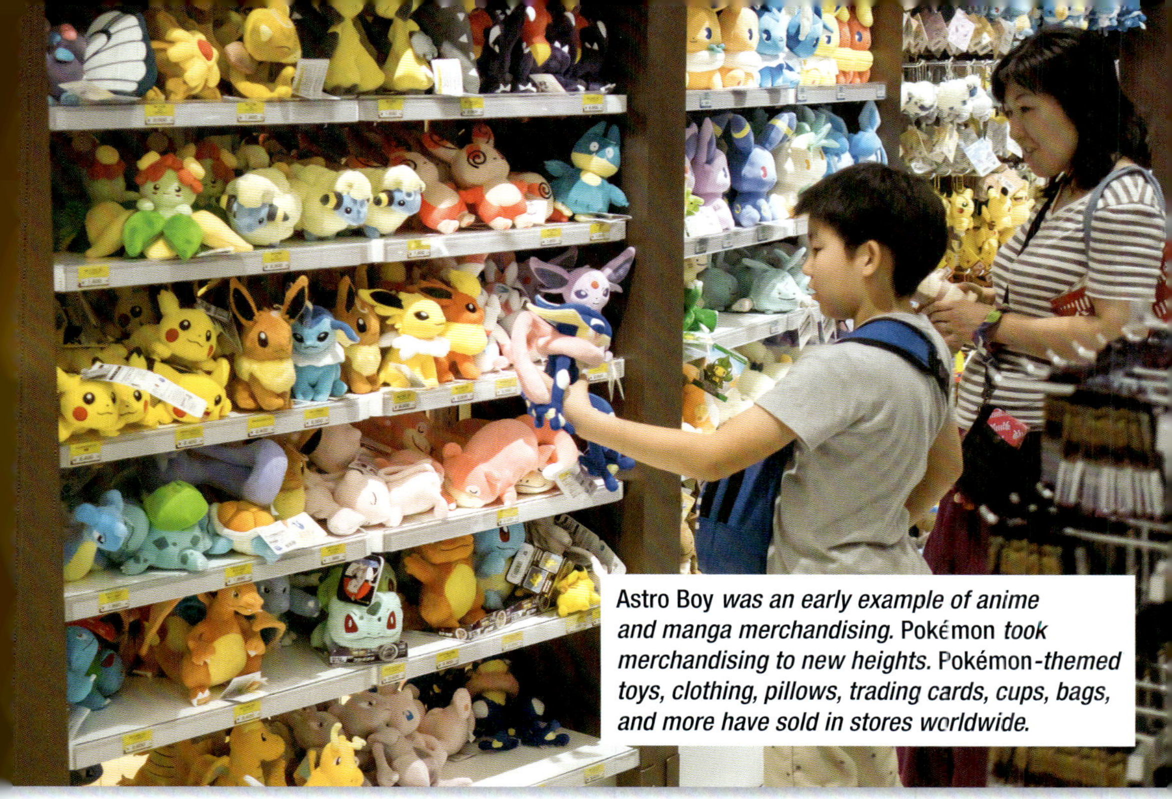

Astro Boy was an early example of anime and manga merchandising. *Pokémon* took merchandising to new heights. *Pokémon*-themed toys, clothing, pillows, trading cards, cups, bags, and more have sold in stores worldwide.

Astro Boy was also one of the earliest examples of anime or manga merchandising, which is the creation of many different types of merchandise related to a particular comic, show, or movie. *Pokémon* is an example of a current anime that has been extensively merchandised. Fans of that show can buy hundreds of different *Pokémon*-related items, including toys, clothing, pillows, trading cards, cups, and bags. At the time that *Astro Boy* was created, though, merchandising was something new. The show's producers were not making enough money to offset production costs, so they licensed the Astro Boy character rights to a confectionary maker, who used the main character on a brand of chocolates.

Anime Flourishes

Following the success of *Astro Boy*, anime took off in Japan. Many new anime started appearing on television, with options for different interests and age groups, including adults. For instance, the 1963 anime *Hermit Village* was on television late at night because it

Doraemon

It was in 1969 that one of Japan's most popular manga premiered. *Doraemon* is about a blue robotic cat that travels back in time from the twenty-second century to help a ten-year old boy named Nobita. Writer Michael Jung explains the story's premise:

> Nobita . . . unfortunately, is terrible in school, clumsy at sports, and regularly bullied by his classmates. . . . Ashamed to have such a loser ancestor, Nobita's great-great-grandson Sewashi Nobi comes up with the idea to send his robot cat Doraemon back in time to look after Nobita when he was a boy. Sewashi hopes that if Doraemon encourages Nobita to stand up for himself and do better in school, history will change and his future descendants' lives will improve.

From this beginning, many adventures follow. Doraemon was so well liked that in 2008, Japan's foreign minister Masahiko Kōmura designated the character as the country's first "animation ambassador," saying, "Doraemon, I hope you will travel around the world as an anime ambassador to deepen people's understanding of Japan so they will become friends with Japan."

Michael Jung, "*Doraemon*: Japan's Best Manga Most Americans Don't Know About," Screen Rant, May 6, 2020. https://screenrant.com.

Quoted in Justin McCurry, "Japan Enlists Cartoon Cat as Ambassador," *The Guardian* (Manchester, UK), March 20, 2008. www.theguardian.com.

was intended for an adult audience. That show is set in an ancient Chinese town where Taoist ascetics abstain from physical pleasures. However, one Taoist student has other ideas; he spends his time chasing after three beautiful girls who live nearby. In 1966 the first animation series targeting young girls was released, called *Sally the Witch*. In it, a witch princess comes to earth by accident but has so much fun that she stays. She tries to keep her magical powers a secret but often ends up getting into mischief. Another popular anime called *Sazae-san* began in 1969. This family show focuses on the life of Japanese homemaker Sazae-san, who lives with her husband, her children, and her parents. While this show has relatively simple plots that focus on everyday life, it has been extremely popular in Japan. In fact, *Sazae-san* is the world's longest-running anime and one of Japan's most successful.

At this time, anime also appeared on television in other countries. *Astro Boy* was one of the first anime to be popular among Western audiences in the United States and Europe. Soon after it aired in Japan, Tezuka made a syndication deal for the show with the NBC network in the United States. This was when he changed the title from *Mighty Atom* to *Astro Boy*. Other anime was exported too—often after being retitled—including *Tetsujin 28-go*, about a boy who controls a giant flying robot, which was renamed *Gigantor*. Tezuka was also asked to create an anime show specifically for US audiences, and he came up with *Kimba the White Lion*. It was created in color. However, while all of these anime shows aired in foreign countries, overall, anime remained relatively unknown outside of Japan.

Manga Grows Too

Like anime, manga continued to become more and more diverse, with artists creating new genres and publishers coming out with new manga magazines. While anyone can read any type of magazine, manga have come to be categorized in a number of different genres based on their target group. *Kodomomuke* manga is intended for young children. Shōnen is aimed at boys from elementary through their late teens, with themes such as action, adventure, sports, and coming of age. Shōjo is for girls and often focuses on romance, comedy, drama, and coming of age. *Seinen* manga is for men, and typical seinen themes are action, crime, violence, business, and sex. Finally, *josei* is for women and is often about family, romance, and sex. However, in addition to these, there are many additional genres and subgenres. For example, *yaoi*, or "boys love," is about romance between two males.

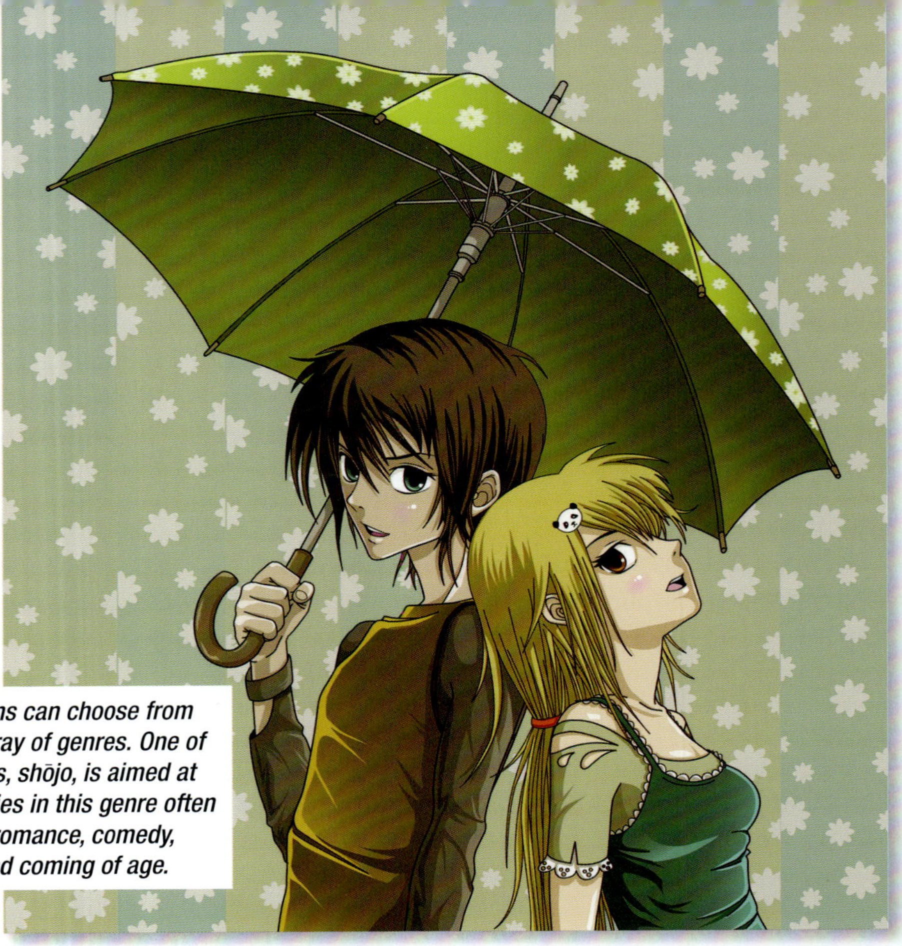

Manga fans can choose from a wide array of genres. One of the genres, shōjo, is aimed at girls; stories in this genre often focus on romance, comedy, drama, and coming of age.

Harem is a type of story where more than one female competes for the attention of one male.

During the 1970s manga for women and girls also became more popular and more varied. Originally, most manga—even that for girls and women—was written by men. Mel, a writer on the manga blog *Hakutaku* explains that while girls and women read these stories, the stories were often missing something because they did not come from a female perspective. She says, "Although girls' interest magazines were popular in the postwar years, many of the manga found in their pages were created by men. While marketable, these manga were often devoid of any deeper meaning; simply cutesy comics to fill up space and make sales."[21] In the 1970s that started to change as more women became manga artists. A group of female artists known as the

Year 24 Group was particularly influential in the creation of manga for girls and women. These women started to explore many new themes in their work, such as gender and sexuality, and they wrote about things that had not been widely discussed before, including lesbian love, teenage pregnancy, and abortion.

"Although girls' interest magazines were popular in the postwar years, many of the manga found in their pages were created by men. While marketable, these manga were often devoid of any deeper meaning."[21]

—Mel, a writer on the manga blog *Hakutaku*

Science fiction manga and anime also became popular in the 1970s, particularly a genre called *mecha*. Writer Amanda Pagan explains this type of story:

> Mecha is a genre of Japanese manga and anime that heavily features or focuses on mechanical innovation. Robots, cyborgs, androids, and space stations, for example, all fall under the wide umbrella of mecha; however, robots are usually the primary focus. The type of robot may vary from series to series, ranging from giant robots used for battle—such as those featured in Yoshiyuki Tomino's *Mobile Suit Gundam*—to more humanoid robots such as Osamu Tezuka's *Astro Boy*.[22]

Mobile Suit Gundam is a show about galactic warfare; it features giant mechanical suits that are controlled by pilots. It was extremely popular and is considered a classic anime show.

Lack of Censorship

Some researchers believe that one thing that helped manga and anime become so diverse was that they were not subject to the same censorship that has occurred in many other countries, meaning that Japanese artists were freer to explore many different kinds of content. Ian Condry, associate professor of comparative media studies, explains that American comic artists initially created a lot of controversial content but were later forced to censor that content. "In the 1940s," Condry states, "American comic books dealt with extreme themes, including gruesome violence and salacious romance. But an uproar surrounding the presumed negative impact on children led a consortium of magazine publishers to establish a Comics Code in 1954 that regulated the content of comic books so they would be appropriate for children."[23] In contrast, says Condry, while there were some protests over controversial content in Japan, there was no similar censorship. In fact, while the United States instituted a code to ensure that comics were appropriate for kids, some Japanese artists created content that was specifically intended for adults—not children.

Another thing that helps maintain the diversity of manga, specifically, is the way the manga industry works in Japan. In many other countries, comics are owned by a publisher. For example, in the United States, DC Comics owns the *Superman* comics. Librarian and manga expert Robin E. Brenner explains that in such a business model, twenty people or more can be involved in creating a comic. She says, "Characters . . . are kept vibrant by moving series from writer to writer and artist to artist with stories that never reach a true end."[24] Critics argue that when comics are controlled by large corporations like this, rather than individuals, there is too much focus on making a profit and less attention to creating an interesting story. In contrast, while manga are also published for profit, they are typically owned and created by a single artist and very focused on telling a particular story. Compared to other comics, manga are a lot more like novels, spread out over numerous volumes with well-developed characters and stories that develop as they progress. And while many manga run for years, most eventually

Anime Cues That Not All Viewers May Understand

A person does not have to know a lot about Japanese culture or anime to appreciate them, but that same person might miss some of what the artist is trying to communicate. This is because anime uses certain symbols and cues to explain some things to the audience without explicitly saying them. Japanese popular culture expert Patrick Drazen gives the example of the *Evangelion* series, in which the droning of cicadas can be heard in many of the outdoor scenes. Drazen explains that "cicadas . . . assert themselves in Japan every summer. However, they are exclusively summer insects. Evangelion features their buzzing week after week, month after month." The year-round presence of these insects has a specific meaning. Drazen continues, "The constant hum of cicadas is a reminder to the viewer (at least, the viewer who knows cicadas) that this is a world in which something has gone horribly wrong."

Patrick Drazen, *Anime Explosion! The What? Why? & Wow! of Japanese Animation.* Berkeley, CA: Stone Bridge, 2003, pp. 20–21.

do have a conclusion. For example, Eiichiro Oda, the creator of *One Piece*—an extremely popular manga that began in 1997—has spoken numerous times about his plans for the series. In 2018, for instance, he warned fans that the story could soon be coming to an end when he said, "The story's about 80% complete."[25]

Manga and anime are constantly evolving, and the 1960s and 1970s were a period of significant change for both of these industries. Television anime went from a nine-minute show about a mole to regular half-hour shows on a huge variety of topics, ranging from robots to magical girls. Manga also increased in diversity, with more and more different magazines and genres catering to all types of interests.

Chapter Four

The Golden Age of Anime and Manga

Dragon Ball is one of the most popular anime and manga of all time. It is about a boy named Son Goku, who trains in martial arts and travels around the world looking for seven orbs, known as Dragon Balls, that can grant him any wish. The first *Dragon Ball* manga was published in 1984, and new series continue to be written. There have also been a number of anime series and movies. *Super Dragon Ball Heroes*, which premiered in 2018, is the most recent television series. A movie—*Dragon Ball Super: Broly*—also came out in 2018. Craig Elvy writes about anime for the entertainment website Screen Rant. He says that many people see *Dragon Ball* as the ultimate example of what manga and anime should be. Says Elvy:

> Because *Dragon Ball* is held in such high esteem, it's often used as the yardstick to measure the success of other anime series, with everyone looking for the "next Dragon Ball." . . . Measured in financial terms or by cultural impact, *Dragon Ball* remains the franchise to beat, but in the modern era, it's highly unlikely any other property, existing or yet to come, will match *Dragon Ball*'s achievements.[26]

Dragon Ball is just one of many manga and anime that began in the 1980s. During the 1980s and 1990s, manga and anime exploded around the world, adding more and more titles and genres and attracting an ever-larger audience. Because anime and manga were so popular during this period, it is often referred to as their "golden age."

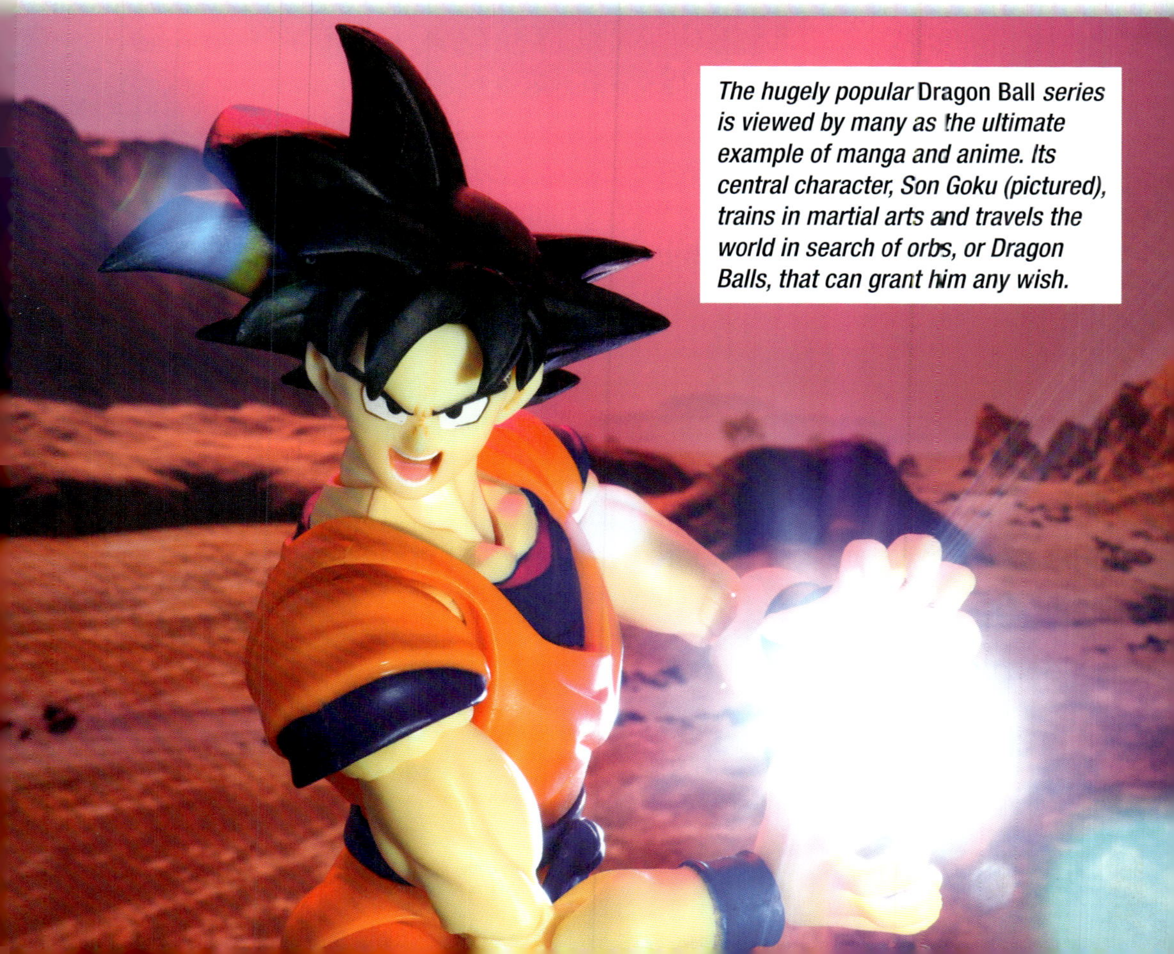

The hugely popular Dragon Ball *series is viewed by many as the ultimate example of manga and anime. Its central character, Son Goku (pictured), trains in martial arts and travels the world in search of orbs, or Dragon Balls, that can grant him any wish.*

Manga Becomes Popular in the United States

While US publishers had been importing manga since the 1960s, through the 1970s mainstream audiences did not take much notice, leaving manga with more of an underground following. That started changing in the 1980s as comic book stores in the United States began stocking translations of popular manga series and titles. But there was one hang-up.

US publishers worried that the Japanese format, which read from right to left, would be too foreign to American readers and would prove to be a drag on expanding the audience. So in the 1980s and 1990s, most manga released in the United States was reformatted to look more like US comics, reading from left to right. This was known as flipping. Unfortunately, sometimes the flipped artwork did not look right or did not make sense. Finally, in 2002 a company called Tokyopop started to publish manga just like it was in Japan, reading from right to left. To help readers who were not familiar with this format, the company added a warning that said, "Stop! This is the back of the book!" so that they would know where to start reading. Sales of the unflipped manga surged, proving that American readers could handle the Japanese style, and other US publishers starting reverting to the original format too.

Akira and the Increasing Popularity of Anime

Anime also became increasingly popular in the United States during the 1980s and 1990s. In 1988, the film *Akira* was released in Japan, and it was shown in many other countries—including the United States—soon after. Set in a dystopian 2019 Tokyo that is full of corruption and violence, the film follows a member of a teenage biker gang as he fights to save his friend from a secret program in which the government is testing psychic children. The film is often referred to as cyberpunk, which is a genre of science fiction that typically focuses on futuristic urban societies that have advanced technology. *Akira* was moderately successful in Japan,

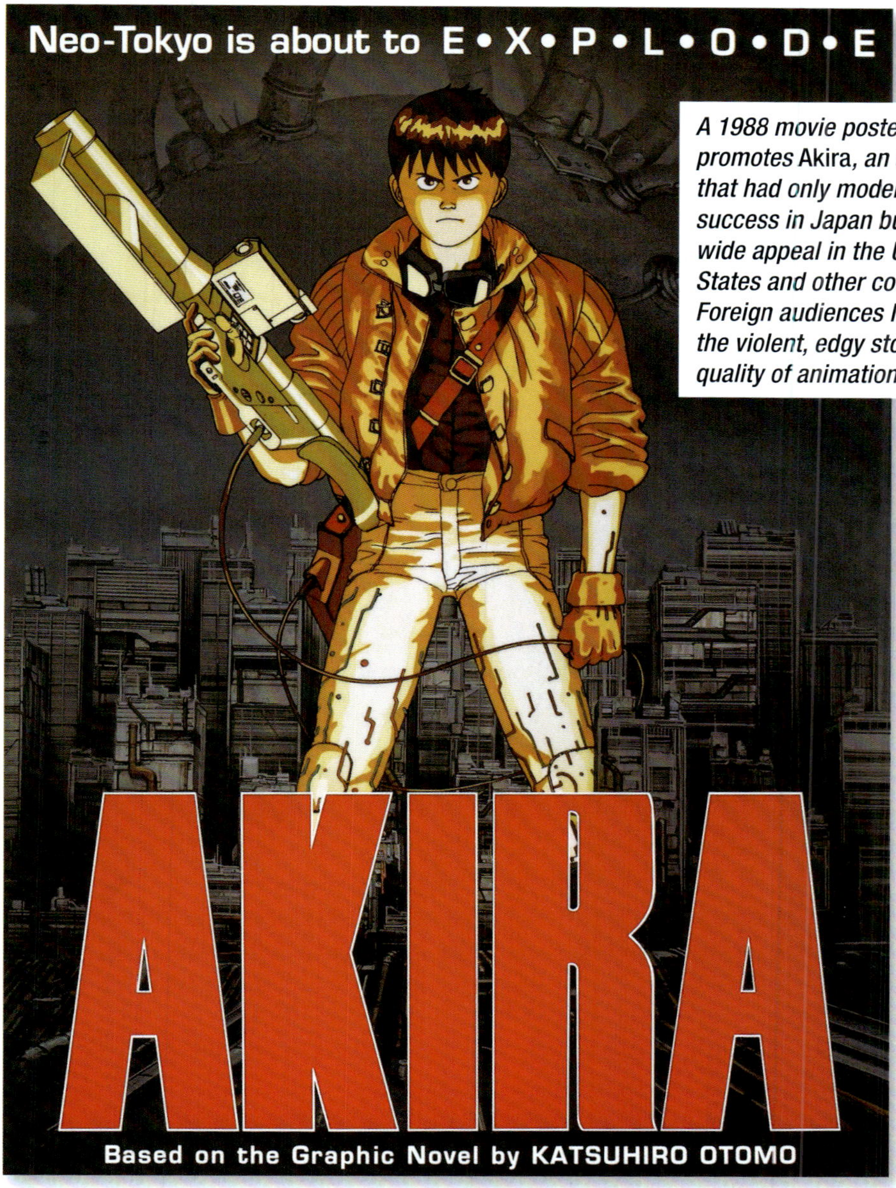

A 1988 movie poster promotes Akira*, an anime that had only moderate success in Japan but gained wide appeal in the United States and other countries. Foreign audiences liked the violent, edgy story and quality of animation.*

but what makes this movie notable in the history of anime is its success outside of Japan. Audiences in the United States and around the world were attracted by the violent, edgy, complex nature of the film, which was something very new for most of them. Many people say that their love of anime started with this film.

Altering Anime for Overseas Markets

During the 1980s anime became increasingly popular outside of Japan. However, as anime expert Simon Richmond explains, it was often altered for non-Japanese audiences in an effort to make it more acceptable and easier to understand. This was often done to the horror of both its creators and its fans, who have argued that these edits ruin it. Richmond gives an example of this editing. He says, "When *Nauiscaä of the Valley of the Wind* made its US debut in 1986, it was in a poorly dubbed version entitled *Warriors of the Wind* that had over thirty minutes hacked from its running time. Many of its key details, including its heroine's name, were altered, watered down or deleted entirely." He says that the film's director was so appalled that it was a whole decade before he was ready to make another deal to distribute one of his films in the United States.

Simon Richmond, *The Rough Guide to Anime: Japan's Finest from Ghibli to Gankutsuō*. New York: Rough Guides, 2009, p. 21.

Akira is also notable for the quality of its animation, which was something many people had never seen before either. *Japan Times* contributing writer Matt Schley explains that *Akira* stood out for the quality of its hand-painted cels and also for the quantity of cels used. He says that by using more frames per second than most other anime, *Akira* was extremely smooth. "Film runs at 24 frames per second, but most anime is shot at 12 or even eight—in other words, the same cel is photographed two or three times in a production method called 'limited animation.' Large chunks of 'Akira,' by contrast, were shot 'on ones,' with each second of footage represented by 24 unique frames. That gave the film an unprecedented fluidity."[27]

Akira attracted a lot of attention to the world of anime and manga in general, and it helped both become much more popular outside of Japan. Journalist Emiko Jozuka explains, "Young

Americans were searching for cultural products offering new perspectives and, to them, Japan appeared to be a place as exciting as 'Akira'—its cyberpunk landscape and controversial plot offering a portal into a different aesthetic and psychological universe."[28] For many Americans, *Akira* was an introduction to the world of anime and manga, and it inspired them to seek out more Japanese comics and animation.

The Magical Girl Genre

In the 1990s one genre of anime and manga that became increasingly popular was something called "magical girl." Quite different from the style of *Akira*, magical girl's popularity came as a result of an anime series called *Sailor Moon*, which premiered in Japan in 1992 and came to the United States in 1995. The magical girl genre is characterized by a seemingly ordinary girl who transforms into a beautiful and superpowered hero in order to fight evil forces. *Sailor Moon*—based on a manga called *Pretty Soldier Sailor Moon*—is about a teenage girl named Usagi Tsukino, who balances everyday life with a destiny to defend the earth as the superpowered warrior Sailor Moon. She does so alongside other girl warriors called the Sailor Scouts. Akiko Sugawa, an associate professor specializing in media and gender studies at Yokohama National University, explains how Sailor Moon exemplifies the magical girl: "She's clumsy. She hates schoolwork. Furthermore, she's bad at sports. In her everyday guise as a schoolgirl, she doesn't exactly shine. But when she summons her magic, she is instantly transformed into an impossibly cute superheroine who battles dauntlessly against monsters and villains."[29] Sugawa says that this is the essence of the magical girl genre.

Sailor Moon became popular with young people—especially girls—all over the world. Patrick Drazen, who lectures on Japanese popular culture, says, "The show's been a hit in Japan, in the U.S. and Canada, in Poland, in the Philippines, in Brazil, and especially on the Internet. Literally hundreds of Web pages sprang up overnight praising one or all of the Sailor Scouts."[30] The original series ran until 1997. There have also been other Sailor Moon series and movies, including *Pretty Guardian Sailor Moon Eternal: The Movie*, which was released in 2021.

Anime Based on Video Games

While many anime are based on manga, some have also been created based on video games. The first was *Super Mario Bros.: The Great Mission to Rescue Princess Peach!*, released in 1996. However, the first anime based on a game that become really successful was *Pokémon*. *Pokémon* (short for "pocket monsters") began as a Nintendo electronic game series that was released in 1996 in Japan and in 1998 in the United States. In the game, players take on the role of Pokémon trainer and must catch monsters and train them to battle other monsters.

The game quickly became extremely popular, and starting in 1997, numerous *Pokémon* movies and TV shows were released. Jozuka writes about just how quickly it became popular, saying, "Pokémon fever swept the globe, triggering a franchise blitz of anime, plushies and trading cards as the bubblegum-yellow Pikachu became a staple on American television sets."[31] The television series has been shown in more than one hundred countries around the world.

"Pokémon fever swept the globe, triggering a franchise blitz of anime, plushies and trading cards as the bubblegum-yellow Pikachu became a staple on American television sets."[31]

—Emiko Jozuka, a journalist

Studio Ghibli

In addition to new anime series and movies, two notable animation studios opened during the 1980s: Studio Ghibli and Gainax.

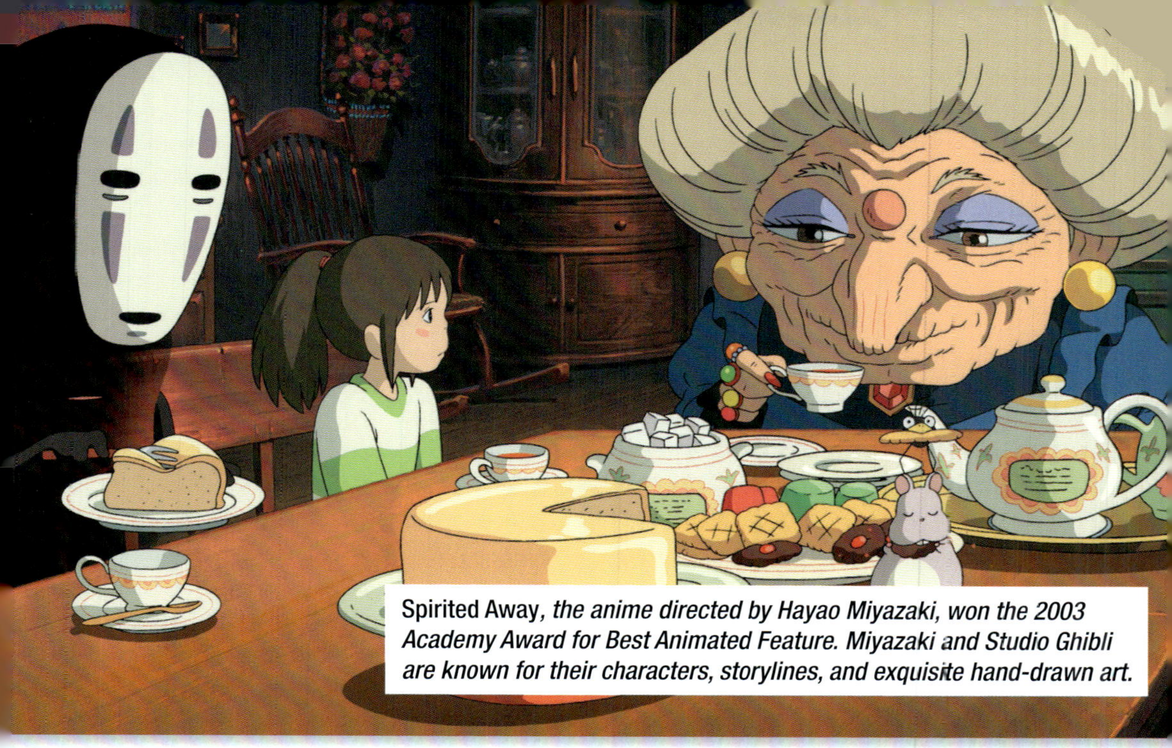

Spirited Away, the anime directed by Hayao Miyazaki, won the 2003 Academy Award for Best Animated Feature. Miyazaki and Studio Ghibli are known for their characters, storylines, and exquisite hand-drawn art.

Studio Ghibli was founded in Tokyo in 1985 by Isao Takahata, Toshio Suzuki, and Hayao Miyazaki. Studio Ghibli, and Miyazaki in particular, are known for producing many successful movies, which have won awards. Miyazaki's characters and storylines, as well as the hand-drawn art, have been very influential in the development of anime. For instance, *Spirited Away*, which was directed by Miyazaki and released in the United States in 2002, is one of Studio Ghibli's best-known releases. This film follows a ten-year-old girl through the spirit world after she gets trapped there. It won numerous awards, including the 2003 Academy Award for Best Animated Feature. Other well-known films produced by Studio Ghibli include *Nausicaa of the Valley of the Wind*, *Laputa: Castle in the Sky*, and *Princess Mononoke*.

Studio Gainax, or just Gainax, was created in 1984 and is also well known for the quality of its animation. One of its most famous releases is the 1995 series *Neon Genesis Evangelion*. This anime is a futuristic story about a group of pilots trying to defend the world from giant machines known as Angels. Part of what makes the series so influential in the world of anime are the themes it deals with. Writers Allegra Frank and Aja Romano explain that *Neon Genesis Evangelion*

> tackles headier concepts: What does it mean to be fighting a battle you don't believe in? When your body becomes a war machine, what will your purpose be when the war is over? If there's a God, why would that God be so cruel to their supposedly beloved creation, humanity? All of these stories and the questions they raise coalesce to become one of the most powerful, visually stunning, intellectually probing anime in the medium's history.[32]

Using Computers in the Animation Process

During the golden age of anime, it became more and more common for animators to use computers to help them do their job. Up until then, they had drawn and colored cels by hand, which was a time-consuming process. Now, with computers, animators were able to scan cels into a computer, then color them and put them together digitally. They started to do so in the 1990s, and by the 2000s most studios had completely switched to digital. One of the last to switch was *Sazae-san*—Japan's longest-running anime and one of its most popular—which eventually made the switch in 2013.

Animators also started to incorporate computer-generated imagery (CGI) into their work. This technology makes it easier to draw very complicated scenes in which there are a lot of details or fast-paced action that would be difficult and time consuming to draw by hand. The first notable use of CGI in an anime film was for *Golgo 13*, released in 1983, about an assassin for hire. The first anime that was created completely with CGI was *A.LI.CE* in 1999. Most anime includes some CGI, usually in addition to hand-drawn cels. CGI does have a major advantage of being much cheaper and quicker than traditional techniques. One anime and manga fan explains in an online article, "Animation is a medium where it takes countless hours of hard work for very little pay. CGI is . . . used to produce

Otaku

A lot of people love to watch anime and read manga, but some fans take their devotion to a different level. *Otaku* is a word that is used for people who become obsessive about their interests. For many otaku, that obsession is manga or anime. These fans are often extremely passionate about a certain manga or anime story or series, and they may know a lot about it and spend large amounts of time reading or watching it. They might also collect toys, pictures, or other things related to their obsession. Many otaku also like to dress up as their favorite manga or anime character. There is a district in Tokyo called Akihabara that has many different establishments that cater to otaku and has become known as a center for otaku culture. According to one travel guide, "Akihabara . . . is famous for the many electronic and Otaku culture shops. From tiny hobby shops to massive department stores specializing in a wide variety of anime, manga, digital entertainment, gadgets, home electronics, general hardware and anything closely related." In addition, Akihabara has a large number of cafés, where visitors can get food and drinks and enjoy manga- and anime-themed decorations and entertainment.

JRPass.com, "The Starting Guidebook to Akihabara, Tokyo," June 25, 2020. www.jrpass.com.

an anime much faster. Instead of hundreds of hours to draw the illustrations and implement them, CGI lets the computer do it. The use of CGI in animation significantly reduces the amount of work needed to produce each episode of an anime."[33] However, while it saves time, many people complain that CGI animation looks unnatural and out of place and is inferior to hand-drawn animation.

While some people did not like the increasing use of CGI, anime and manga remained extremely popular at the end of the twentieth century and into the twenty-first. Not only did they remain a staple form of entertainment in Japan, they also finally moved outside of Japan. Finally, anime and manga had found a solid base of fans in countries around the world, including the United States.

Chapter Five

Anime and Manga Today

One of the most popular manga series of all time is called *One Piece*. Written by Eiichiro Oda, this manga began in 1997 and is ongoing. It follows the adventures of a pirate named Monkey D. Luffy, who—after eating the magical gum-gum fruit—can stretch his body like rubber. Luffy and his crew travel around the world in search of a mysterious treasure called the One Piece. In early 2021 *One Piece* achieved two major milestones: it published its one thousandth chapter, and it reached a total of 480 million copies in circulation worldwide. *One Piece* is just one of many manga and anime that are eagerly followed by millions of fans. As they have throughout history, both manga and anime continue to evolve and to face challenges, but they also remain very popular.

Recent Sales Trends

In the United States sales of both manga and anime have been surging in recent years. The market research company NPD Group reports, "Interest in manga and anime-influenced content reached an all-time high in 2020."[34] The company says that in the United States, three of the top ten animated series for kids in 2020 were anime style, and manga was one of the fastest-growing categories of books for adults. Netflix, which offers numerous anime for streaming—including the popular *Demon Slayer* series—reports that there was a 100 percent rise in anime watching in 2020, compared to 2019.

> **"Interest in manga and anime-influenced content reached an all-time high in 2020."[34]**
>
> **—NPD Group, a market research company**

While manga and anime sales have been surging in the United States and many other countries in the past fifteen years, they have actually been in decline in Japan. Some people blame the decline on online piracy, which has reduced profits. Others say that the quality of manga and anime has deteriorated, with more

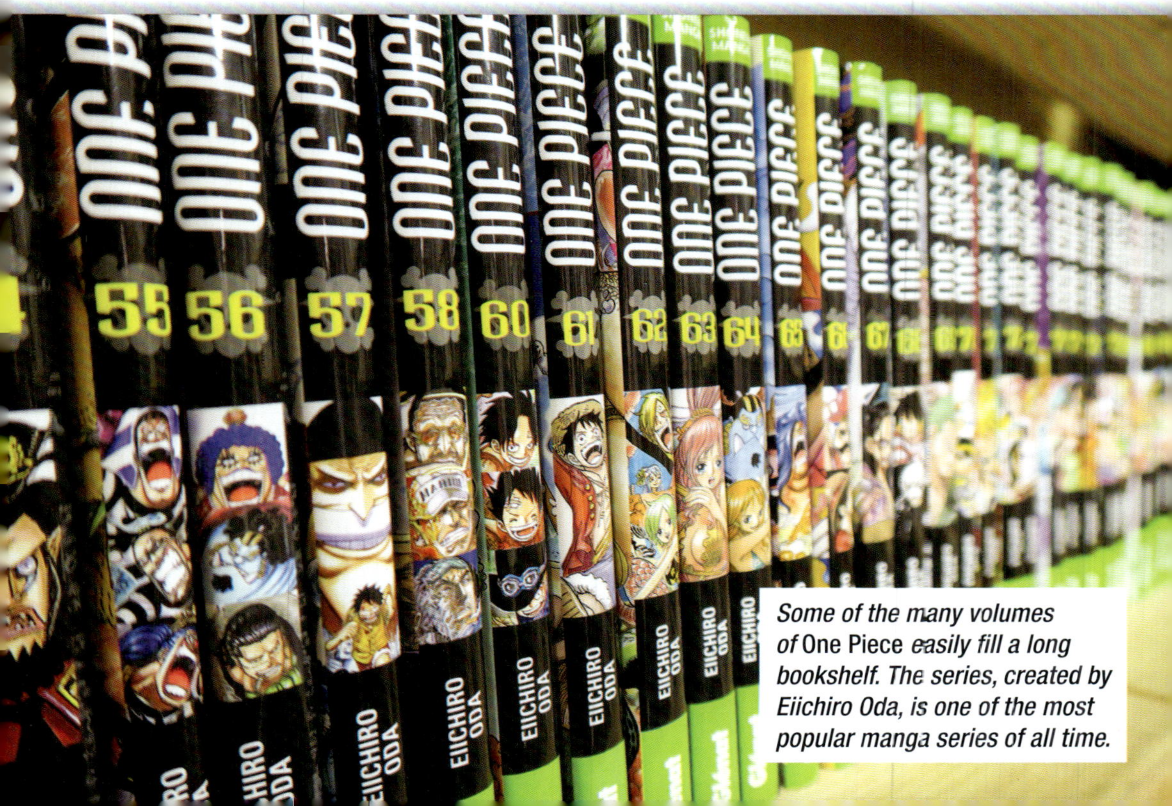

Some of the many volumes of One Piece *easily fill a long bookshelf. The series, created by Eiichiro Oda, is one of the most popular manga series of all time.*

focus on marketing and less focus on continuing to create interesting and complex stories. However, even with lower sales, the overall size of Japan's manga and anime markets remain significant, and in 2020 both actually increased for the first time in many years. The Association of Japanese Animations provides some statistics on these trends. It reports that the Japanese anime market hit a peak in 2014, then shrunk until 2019, when it then saw an increase of 15 percent. There was also a big increase in manga sales in 2020. Many people believe these increases are due to the fact that people spent so much time at home in 2020 as a result of the COVID-19 pandemic.

What Makes Manga and Anime So Popular?

More than one hundred years after the first manga were read and the first anime were watched, these forms of art and entertainment continue to be very popular. Some people believe that one reason for their popularity within Japan is that they offer people an escape from the conformity that is strongly encouraged in Japanese society. While some other countries, such as the United States, encourage individualism, Japanese society often pressures its citizens to conform to the status quo and follow the norms of their group. For example, most schools have strict regulations about how students must dress and even how they can style their hair. Susan J. Napier teaches Japanese literature and culture at the University of Texas at Austin. She believes that anime, with its characters that look completely different from the way most people do in Japan, allow the Japanese people a safe way to temporarily escape from conformity and can help them un-

"The anime medium—precisely because it so often highlights characters and settings that are neither clearly Western nor clearly Japanese—offers a space for identity expression."[35]

—Susan J. Napier, who teaches Japanese literature and culture at the University of Texas at Austin

Manga Cafés

One way to read manga in Japan is to go to a manga café. A manga café has a large library of manga for visitors to read. These cafés also offer numerous amenities such as internet access, drinks, pay showers, vending machines, and private rooms. Visitors pay based on how long they stay and what type of amenities they use. Many manga cafés are open twenty-four hours a day, and some people even sleep there. Blogger Christine Kaaloa stayed at a manga café when she had an airport layover and did not want to pay for a hotel. She says, "Each compartment was separated by closing doors and the noise volume in the cafe was similar to a library." She chose a compartment with a lounge recliner and says it was comfortable to sleep in. Of the compartment, she says, "It certainly felt more personal and private than a dorm room in a hostel. I had my very own space. I could store my bags, I had a place to hang my coat and I had my own computer, TV and charging station. All mine." Overall, she says it was a very good experience.

Christine Kaaloa, "A Night at the Coolest Budget Stay in Japan . . . the Manga Cafe," *GRRRL TRAVELER*, 2008. https://grrrltraveler.com.

derstand what it might feel like to take on a different identity. She says, "The anime medium—precisely because it so often highlights characters and settings that are neither clearly Western nor clearly Japanese—offers a space for identity expression in which the audience can revel in a safe form of otherness unmatched by any other contemporary medium."[35] Manga too, offers readers an escape from everyday life, with its colorful characters and fantastic plots.

Yet, while manga and anime may offer the Japanese people an escape from everyday life, at the same time, they contain a lot of images from everyday life in Japan. For many people who do not live in the country, these details are precisely what makes them so appealing. Anime expert Simon Richmond explains, "For many overseas fans what makes anime cool is . . . its otherness—

> **"For many overseas fans what makes anime cool is . . . its otherness—that it stems from a culture different from their own."[36]**
>
> —Simon Richmond, an expert on anime

that it stems from a culture different from their own. Japanese language, culture and modes of behavior—everything from the differences in the schooling system to what people eat for breakfast—permeate anime, adding depth and nuance."[36]

Young people who read manga and watch anime often become so engaged by this otherness that they are inspired to learn more about Japanese culture. Says librarian and manga expert Robin E. Brenner, "These readers research mythology and history; discuss the details of the plot, costume, and acts of cultural significance; learn to read, write, and speak Japanese; long to visit the shrines and bustling cities of Japan; and mine each volume for information about the story, place, and period. They decipher each new symbol or reference they don't know . . . and try to figure out why their own sense of humor is different from the writers and readers in Japan."[37]

Critiques of Manga and Anime

However, while manga and anime are very popular around the world, they are also controversial. Some critics argue that they often contain content that is harmful to certain people. For instance, a common critique is that a significant number of anime and manga give unhealthy messages about how women should be treated. Writer Jenna Mayzouni talks about the treatment of women in shōjo manga, which are manga that are aimed at young female readers. She says that many of these manga portray abusive relationships, in which women are expected to be submissive to men, sometimes subject to sexual assault, and often blamed for being the victim. For example, Mayzouni says, "In many manga series, men rape women as a form of revenge against another male character. And, despite the horror and malice of the act, the heroines forgive them more often than not." She worries about the implications of this, saying:

> The thing is, [shōjo] manga specifically targets young girls starting to develop their views on sexuality and relationships. Consistently encountering manga . . . [that shows this kind of treatment of women] instead of healthier romances and relationships . . . can be really unhealthy for many of these girls, especially if they don't have any adults in their lives to help them talk about or discuss the problems in those relationships.[38]

Mayzouni believes that women who read a lot of this type of manga may come to believe that abusive relationships such as this are normal.

Some critics also argue that a lot of manga and anime is very violent, and they believe that this can have a negative effect on readers and viewers, such as making them more likely to think that violence is okay or do violent things themselves in real life. A man named Tsutomu Miyazaki was convicted of murdering four girls in Tokyo during 1988 to 1999, and some people believed that he was influenced by violent anime. He was nicknamed the "Otaku Killer" because of his fascination with anime and the large collection of anime that was found in his apartment after his arrest.

However, others insist that many manga and anime actually contain lots of positive messages. For example, writer Claudia Besant describes five manga that portray strong and self-confident women. In the series *Stray God*, one of the main characters is Hiyori. Besant says:

> Hiyori is a defiant, tenacious, and selfless character, challenging typical [shōnen] tropes and limiting gender roles. Her secret love for professional martial arts, something deemed "unfeminine" by her parents and friends, reveals

> her desire to break free from stereotypes and societal pressure to conform. . . . Throughout the series, Hiyori repeatedly saves . . . characters and is shown gratitude and respect in return, subverting the common passive, damsel in distress trope.[39]

Another example of a positive influence is the anime *Naruto*. Rock Lee is one of the main characters in *Naruto*. Unlike most of his peers, he is not able to use *ninjutsu* or *genjutsu* fighting techniques, and he has to put in a lot more hard work than the other characters in order to become a good fighter. It is argued that Rock Lee teaches viewers the importance of perseverance and hard work.

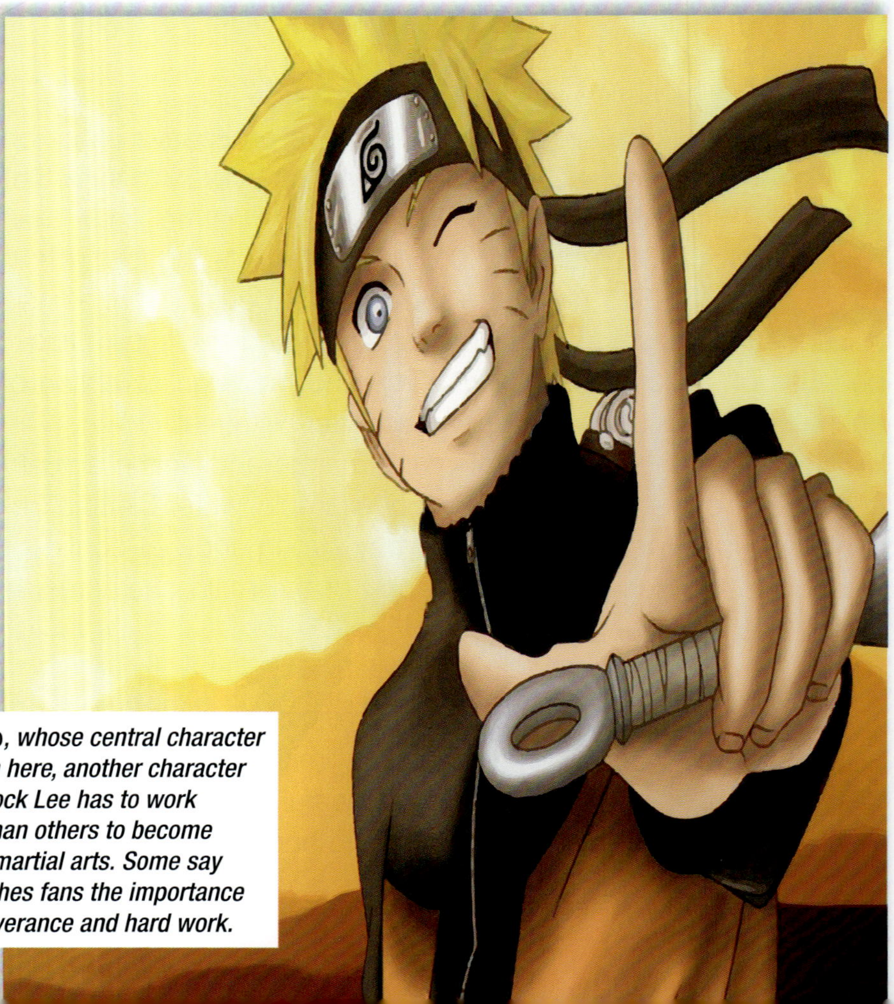

In Naruto*, whose central character is shown here, another character called Rock Lee has to work harder than others to become good at martial arts. Some say this teaches fans the importance of perseverance and hard work.*

Anime and Manga Artists Often Work Long Hours

No matter what kind of lesson a manga or anime teaches, creating it is a lot of work. Both industries are notorious for the hard work required of their artists. For instance, manga editor Jason Thompson says that many manga artists have very little free time or even time to sleep. He says, "Some manga artists go days without sleep to meet their deadlines, and burnout horror stories abound."[40]

In an interview, manga artist Hiro Mashima talks about how long it takes to sketch just one chapter of his manga, *Fairy Tail*. He says, "It takes about five days. On Monday, I work on the script and storyboards. On Tuesday, I work on the rough sketches. Then Wednesday through Friday, I finish the drawing and inking. On the other two days, I work on *Monster Hunter*, which is a monthly series for Shonen Rival. I work on a quarter of the story each weekend, and by the end of the month, I've finished a chapter."[41] Manga artists usually have assistants to help them meet their deadlines; however, even with help, most still work extremely long hours.

The anime industry is also known for how hard its artists work. In addition, there is widespread criticism that while the anime business is lucrative, those profits go to the animation studios, while the animators themselves receive very little money for all of their work. For example, for a recent *New York Times* article, the writers spoke to Tetsuya Akutsu, who has been an animator in Japan for eight years. They report, "He takes home just $1,400 to $3,800 a month as a top animator and an occasional director on some of Japan's most popular anime franchises. And he is one of the lucky ones: Thousands of lower-rung illustrators do grueling piecework for as little as $200 a month."[42] Akutsu says that while he would like to continue working in the anime industry for the rest of his life, he realizes that he cannot do so if he wants to get married and have a child, because his income is simply not enough.

The Impact of the Internet

Manga and anime artists have also been affected by the popularity of the internet in recent years. This technology has made it much easier for these creations to be shared without the owner's permission. Before the internet, fans had to buy the manga or anime that they wanted. For example, they could purchase manga in a bookstore. Now it is easy to find a huge variety of manga and anime content online, completely free. Unfortunately, in most cases it is posted there without the owner's permission, and that owner does not receive any money when other people watch or read his or her work. In the case of manga, when a person scans, translates, and posts a story online like this, it is referred to as a "scanlation." An editorial in the art magazine *Widewalls* explains, "With scanlations appearing sometimes mere hours after a new chapter is released in Japan, the practice is striking at the heart of manga and threatening its very existence. This is making it increasingly difficult for manga artists, or mangaka, to earn a living from their work."[43]

However, the internet has had positive effects too. It has helped anime and manga become more popular because it has given fans access to a much wider range of content. Anime fan Michelle Villanueva talks about watching anime before the internet existed. She says that before the internet, if you wanted to watch an anime show, you had to either watch it on television, rent it, or buy it. With either of those options, there was only a limited number of titles available, and buying was expensive, she says. The existence of the internet and streaming has meant much more variety. Villanueva explains:

> While the market in the past relied on series which were successful (everyone likes giant robots, right?) and ignored titles which piqued niche interests, streaming makes distribution cheap enough to allow for more series to be featured. Want a show about teen friendship? Check. A show about girls wanting to become pop idols? Tons of those. A show about a high school boys swim club? Oh . . . yes.[44]

Unpredictable Plots

The characters and plots in anime and manga are often far more complex and less predictable than other types of comics and animation, and that makes them more interesting to many fans. For example, manga editor Jason Thompson points out that while manga and anime characters often have superpowers or fantasy lives, they are also real people who have real-life responsibilities and character flaws. He says:

> Even in worlds that exist in the far future, or long ago, the reader is drawn into a 3-dimensional character, one who is far from perfect, one who has stupid little habits or major character flaws—and who has hopes and dreams that the reader can sympathize with. Unlike some American super heroes, who often seem to just go around defeating Evil . . . Japanese characters usually have other goals in life that play large themes within their lives.

Manga expert Simon Richmond says anime and manga have similar qualities. "Compared to your average Hollywood animated product," he points out, "anime are far more complex, and less likely to have clear-cut heroes and villains, or to stick to absolute definitions of right and wrong—let alone feature a happy, neatly wrapped-up ending."

Jason Thompson, *Manga: The Complete Guide*. New York: Ballantine, 2007, p. xx.

Simon Richmond, *The Rough Guide to Anime: Japan's Finest from Ghibli to Gankutsuō*. New York: Rough Guides, 2009, p. vii.

Despite the threat of piracy and the critiques related to content, manga and anime continue to inspire millions of fans around the world. Timothy Perper and Martha Cornog, editors of an anthology of essays about manga and anime, comment that it comes down to the fact there is something unique and compelling about these forms of art and entertainment that people fall in love with. They observe that "manga and anime have worldwide influence and appeal. It's not hard, not really, to explain why—they contain some of the finest storytelling and most beautiful artwork in the modern world."[45]

Source Notes

Introduction: Unlike Anything Else

1. Susan J. Napier, *Anime: From Akira to Princess Mononoke; Experiencing Contemporary Japanese Animation*. Palgrave: New York, 2001, pp. 19–20.
2. Napier, *Anime*, pp. 6–7.
3. Patrick Drazen, *Anime Explosion! The What? Why? & Wow! of Japanese Animation*. Berkeley, CA: Stone Bridge, 2003, p. 21.
4. Japan House Los Angeles, "Drawn to Inspire: The Impact of Manga and Anime," August 16, 2016. www.japanhousela.com.

Chapter One: Early Anime and Manga

5. Napier, *Anime*, p. 7.
6. Robin E. Brenner, *Understanding Manga and Anime*. Westport, CT: Libraries Unlimited, 2007, p. 2.
7. Rising Sun Prints, "One Piece and Ukiyo-E: Drawing Inspiration from Edo Japan," November 28, 2019. https://risingsunprints.com.
8. Christy C., "A Brief History of Japanese Comics Part 6: 60's and 70's—a Modernizing Age," *A Scroll in Time* (blog), December 10, 2016. http://ascrollintime.blogspot.com.
9. Right Stuf Anime, "The History of Anime," Right Stuf Inc. www.rightstufanime.com.
10. Liana Sharer, "The Beginnings of Anime and Manga," That Anime Project, 2001. http://umich.edu.

Chapter Two: Development After World War II

11. Brenner, *Understanding Manga and Anime*, pp. 5–6.
12. Tabatha Butler, "How Walt Disney Influenced Anime," *The Movie Blog*, August 19, 2013. www.themovieblog.com.

13. Quoted in Heidi Kemps, "Interview: Akihiro Kanayama," Anime News Network, September 1, 2014. www.animenewsnetwork.com.
14. Grace Zeigler, "A Brief History of Anime and Manga: From Zen Cartoons to *Sailor Moon*," AnimeChicago, April 20, 2017. https://animechicago.com.
15. Frederik L. Schodt, "A Word from the Translator," in *The Osamu Tezuka Story: A Life in Manga and Anime*, by Toshio Ban and Tezuka Productions. Berkeley, CA: Stone Bridge, 2016, p. viii.
16. Christy C., "A Brief History of Japanese Comics Part 6."
17. Yamaguchi Yasuo, "The Evolution of the Japanese Anime Industry," Nippon.com, December 20, 2013. www.nippon.com.
18. Washi, "The Start of the Anime Industry—Toei Douga & *Hakujaden*," *Washi's Blog*, November 30, 2018. https://washiblog.wordpress.com.

Chapter Three: Growth During the 1960s and 1970s

19. Right Stuf Anime, "The History of Anime."
20. Right Stuf Anime, "The History of Anime."
21. Mel, "The Magnificent, Revolutionary Year 24 Group," *Hakutaku* (blog), July 17, 2018. www.hakutaku.us.
22. Amanda Pagan, "A Beginner's Guide to Mecha," New York Public Library, April 4, 2019. www.nypl.org.
23. Ian Condry, *The Soul of Anime*. Durham, NC: Duke University Press, 2013, p. 21.
24. Brenner, *Understanding Manga and Anime*, p. 14.
25. Eiichiro Oda, interviewed by Yayoi Kawatoko, "'Luffy Is My Ideal Child' Says *One Piece* Author, Eiichiro Oda," *Edomongatari,* July 24, 2018. https://edomonogatari.wordpress.com/2018/07/24/yomiuri-oda.

Chapter Four: The Golden Age of Anime and Manga

26. Craig Elvy, "No Other Anime Will Ever Emulate *Dragon Ball's* Success," Screen Rant, February 13, 2020. https://screenrant.com.
27. Matt Schley, "Collecting 'Akira,' One Scene at a Time," *Japan Times*. https://features.japantimes.co.jp.
28. Emiko Jozuka, "Japanese Anime: From 'Disney of the East' to a Global Industry Worth Billions," CNN, July 28, 2019. www.cnn.com.
29. Sugawa Akiko, "Children of Sailor Moon: The Evolution of Magical Girls in Japanese Anime," Nippon.com, February 26, 2015. www.nippon.com.
30. Drazen, *Anime Explosion!*, p. 11.
31. Jozuka, "Japanese Anime."
32. Allegra Frank and Aja Romano, "8 Things to Know About *Neon Genesis Evangelion*, the Legendary Anime Now Streaming on Netflix," Vox, June 21, 2019. www.vox.com.

33. Mahapatra, "What Is CGI in Anime? Why Is It Used? Is It Good or Bad?," Animehunch, March 23, 2021. https://animehunch.com.

Chapter Five: Anime and Manga Today

34. NPD Group, "Manga and Anime: The Latest Annual Insights." www.npd.com.
35. Napier, *Anime*, p. 27.
36. Simon Richmond, *The Rough Guide to Anime: Japan's Finest from Ghibli to Gankutsuō*. New York: Rough Guides, 2009, p. vii.
37. Brenner, *Understanding Manga and Anime*, p xii.
38. Jenna Mayzouni, "Harmful Gimmick: The Normalization of Abuse in Shoujo Manga," Anime Feminist, May 8, 2019. www.animefeminist.com.
39. Claudia Besant, "5 Manga Featuring Self-Willed Female Protagonists," Books & Bao, February 22, 2021. https://booksandbao.com.
40. Thompson, *Manga*, p. xxi.
41. Quoted in Deb Aoki, "Interview with Manga Artist Hiro Mashima," LiveAbout, February 11, 2019. www.liveabout.com.
42. Ben Dooley and Hikari Hida, "Anime Is Booming. So Why Are Animators Living in Poverty?," *New York Times*, February 24, 2021. www.nytimes.com.
43. Widewalls Editorial, "A Short History of Manga," *Widewalls*, September 24, 2016. www.widewalls.ch.
44. Michelle Villanueva, "Technology and Anime, a Beautiful Love Story," Mary Sue, June 4, 2014. www.themarysue.com.
45. Timothy Perper and Martha Cornog, eds., *Mangatopia: Essays on Manga and Anime in the Modern World*. Santa Barbara, CA: Libraries Unlimited, 2011, p. 238.

For Further Research

Books

Matt Alt, *Pure Invention: How Japan's Pop Culture Conquered the World*. New York: Crown, 2020.

Patrick Drazen, *Anime Explosion! The What? Why? & Wow! of Japanese Animation*. Berkeley, CA: Stone Bridge, 2014.

Hector Garcia, *A Geek in Japan: Discovering the Land of Manga, Anime, Zen, and the Tea Ceremony*. North Clarendon, VT: Tuttle, 2019.

Robert M. Henderson, *Quick Guide to Anime and Manga*. San Diego, CA: ReferencePoint, 2022.

Maria Roberta Novielli, *Floating Worlds: A Short History of Japanese Animation*. Boca Raton, FL: CRC, 2018.

Chris Stuckman, *Anime Impact: The Movies and Shows That Changed the World of Japanese Animation*. Coral Gables, FL: Mango, 2018.

Internet Sources

Charlie Horner, "What Is the History of Anime in Japan?," *Japan Junky*, 2020. www.japanjunky.com.

Right Stuf Anime, "The History of Anime," Right Stuf Inc. www.rightstufanime.com.

Eric Shorey, "Manga vs. Anime: A Brief History of the Two Mediums," *ONE37pm*, February 23, 2021. www.one37pm.com.

Widewalls Editorial, "A Short History of Manga," *Widewalls*, September 24, 2016. www.widewalls.ch.

Yamaguchi Yasuo. "The Evolution of the Japanese Anime Industry," Nippon.com, December 20, 2013. www.nippon.com.

Index

ESSEX PUBLIC LIBRARY
000233603